Romanticism Reborn

Ayn Rand, 20th Century Romanticism,

and Romantic Realism.

_____

By Walter Donway

The Atlas Society Press

Published by The Atlas Society Press
800 Rockmead Drive, Suite 200
Kingwood, TX 77339

Romanticism Reborn is a new Atlas Society edition of the book originally independently under the title, *Ayn Rand's Road to Romanticism.*

Cover design by Matthew Holdridge
Book layout by Erin Redding and Lorence Olivo
Proof Editing by Donna Paris

AtlasSociety.org

ISBN: 978-1-7349605-9-4

Our Mission

The Atlas Society's mission is to inspire people to embrace reason, achievement, benevolence and ethical self-interest as the moral foundation for political liberty, personal happiness and a flourishing society.

We build on Ayn Rand's works and ideas, and use artistic and other creative means to reach and inspire new audiences. We promote an open and empowering brand of Objectivism; we welcome engagement with all who honestly seek to understand the philosophy, and we use reason, facts and open debate in the search for truth above all else; we do not appeal to authority or conflate personalities with ideas. We resist moral judgment without adequate facts, and believe disagreement does not necessarily imply evasion.

Dedicated:

*To the Future of Romanticism
and its incomparable potential
to lift and ennoble man's spirit.*

Other books by Walter Donway

Novels
The Way the Wind Blew
The Price of Hannah Blake
The Lailly Worm
O Human Child
Tarzan in the Heart of Darkness
Retaking College Hill

Nonfiction
Not Half Free: The Myth that America Is Capitalist
Donald Trump and His Enemies: How the Media Put Trump in Office
Media Wars: The Battle to Shape Our Minds (with Vinay Kolhatkar)

Poetry
Touched by Its Rays
How Glad I Am for Man, Tonight
Speak Their Names, Once More

Memoirs
"You're Probably from Holden, If...: Growing Up in A Vanishing New England"
"You're Probably from Worcester, if..."

Contents

Preface to Romanticism Reborn

David Kelley

Walter Donway is a prolific writer, with many works of fiction and nonfiction to his credit. In this volume, he turns to his major passion: the power of art, especially literature—and Romantic literature in particular—to portray a life-changing and inspiring moral ideal.

The articles that make up this collection were composed at different times and published in different venues, which results in some repetition among them. But I found the repetition useful in making important points memorable. Some originated as talks, retaining the informal style of address to an audience. This, too, contributes to the enjoyment of his book: Overall, it has the feel of a great conversation or college seminar with an expert who can present deep insights in accessible form.

Walter traces his understanding of the power of art to Ayn Rand and her novel *Atlas Shrugged.*, telling us about the impact it had on him as a young man and its continuing impact throughout his life. The chapter "Incurable Atlas Fever" is a beautifully written autobiographical account of his discovery of the novel. "*Atlas Shrugged*, in a sense, slid like a key into a lock with the answer to the puzzle of my Romantic longing." That gives this work a personal feel that is moving, and that I hope other fans of *Atlas* can relate to.

But the book goes far beyond the personal. The main theme is Romanticism: its nature, history, and varieties, with discussions of many historical and contemporary works in the genre. Walter refers often to Rand's *Romantic Manifesto*, with illuminating observations drawn from his deep understanding of her Objectivist philosophy. But he goes far beyond Rand's book in his detailed treatment of the Romantic movement. Even those well-versed in Objectivism will find arresting insights and applications.

The book begins with two of the longer essays that provide context for the other pieces. In "The Romantic Revolution: The Glory, the Paradoxes, the Future," Donway discusses the history of Romanticism and the paradox it represents. Those who began their intellectual journey with Rand's novels and non-fiction works may take her esthetic theory as totally consistent with her broader philosophy. And it is.

But most intellectual historians consider the Romanticism of the early 19ᵗʰ century a rejection of the Enlightenment. It was indeed a rejection of the Classicism typical of Enlightenment aesthetics, with its fixed standards for the form of art works—like the classical standards for architecture that Roark battles against in *The Fountainhead*. Historians, however, usually regard the Romantic movement as a broader rejection of Enlightenment ideas and values. Many Romantic novelists and poets celebrated feeling and intuition over reason. They looked back to folklore, myths, and the Middle Ages rather than the new world of capitalism and industry. Many of them turned away from these man-made advances to celebrate Nature. How then can Objectivism—an Enlightenment philosophy—embrace Romanticism in art? Consider, for example, William Wordworth's poem "The World Is Too Much With Us":

The world is too much with us; late and soon,
Getting and spending, we lay waste our powers:
Little we see in Nature that is ours…

How can that Romantic poem, with its rejection of commerce in favor of Nature, be part of the same artistic genre as the capitalist ideal in *Atlas Shrugged*?

Walter's answer, in brief, is that Romanticism completed the Enlightenment's project of liberating the individual. His analysis is a tour-de-force, integrating the historical evolution of Romanticism with a deep and original view of Rand's concept of "sense of life" and the role of art in finding "the homeland of one's soul." This essay alone, in my view, is worth the price of the book.

The second chapter, "*Atlas Shrugged* Resuscitates Dying Romanticism," covers some of the same ground as the first but goes deeper into Rand's theory of literature, her opposition to Naturalism (or Realism), the philosophical ideas that undermined Romanticism in the 19ᵗʰ and 20ᵗʰ centuries, the differences between popular and literary Romanticism, and the way *Atlas Shrugged* offers the deepest, most consistent, portrayal of the Romantic focus on individual choice and commitment to values.

Walter argues here that the "resuscitation of Romanticism—in the form of Romantic Realism—was Ayn Rand's single most original philosophical achievement," more significant than her insights in epistemology or ethics. As a philosopher who has written a good deal about her break-through insights in those fields, I can't agree. But Walter's argument for the claim is intriguing and invites further reflection.

Romanticism Reborn goes on to discuss a number of specific works in depth, including Tolstoy's *War and Peace* and Dumas's *The Count of Monte Cristo*. To my mind, the most interesting are the two chapters devoted to Henryk Sienkiewicz, the Polish author of the immensely popular *Quo Vadis?* That novel depicts the struggles of the earliest Christians in Rome during Emperor Nero's reign; Ayn Rand considered it in the top rank of Romantic novels. But Sienkiewicz is more celebrated in Poland for his "Trilogy," three novels of Poland's struggles against invaders in the 17th century. The trilogy was completed in 1887 but translated into English only in 1991. "The great universal themes of the Trilogy," Walter says,

> are that no nation survives loss of its founding ideas and values, and that the salvation of a nation ultimately lies in the mind of each citizen.
> Notable glories of the books are the portrayal of courage, comradeship, and valor in war; achingly intense and beautiful romance; depth of analysis of the moral corruption that brings a great country to enslavement; and the blazingly colorful, complex characters and their moral grandeur.

A later chapter, "The Great Romantic Novel You Haven't Read," covers Sienkiewicz's *The Knights of the Cross*. Like most readers, as Walter's title surmises, I haven't read the novel. It's on my list now.

What about contemporary novels? Popular Romanticism, of course, survives in many forms: detective stories, thrillers, and much science fiction. They count as Romantic because they involve heroes fighting for their values, but, as Walter notes, they "all deal with values mostly in terms of crime and punishment or good agents versus malefactors." Yet Walter comments extensively ("What Is Romanticism, Today?") on current popular novels, including a new wave of fantasy and young adult fiction, selecting his favorites.

In another chapter on contemporary writers inspired by Rand, Walter singles out several authors whose novels rise above the popular level, Vinay Kolhatkar and D.K. Halling, with extended discussions of their works. (A fuller list of such authors was compiled by Marilyn Moore for The Atlas Society website: "Fiction Under the Influence: Ayn Rand's Literary Legacy," https://www.atlassociety.org/post/fiction-under-the-influence-ayn-rands-literary-legacy.)

Finally, the book includes two great chapters on poetry. Rand did not have a lot to say about the genre, though she requested that a poem, Rudyard Kipling's "If," be read at her funeral (another Kipling poem was read for her husband Frank O'Connor). In any case, Walter is an accomplished poet himself, with extensive knowledge about the history of the genre. "Who Stole Poetry and Left Us Only Free Verse?" begins with a humorous description of his experience in poetry workshops where most of the participants offer "free verse." The problem is that "free verse is not poetry"; free verse dispenses with meter, the regular patterns of stress in each line, and meter is the defining characteristic of poetry.

Walter expands on that point in a longer chapter that includes a tutorial on the varieties of meter and their artistic effects, for those of us who have forgotten the differences among iambic, anapestic, and other meters that we learned about in school (when schools still taught this material).

This chapter also makes the bold claim in its title, "Poetry: The Supreme Art." Fasten your seat belt for Walter's argument that poetry is supreme because it includes elements of every other form of art, from dance to painting. In aid of his argument, he reminds us that poetry is not limited to the short lyric form we are familiar with today. Much of the great literature in Western history was in verse—from the epics of Homer to Virgil's Aeneid, to Dante's Divine Comedy, to Shakespeare's plays, to mention just a few.

These chapters are a testament to the immense power of poetry, to its glorious history—and to the depth of Walter's love for this art.

But enough from me: It's time for you to explore the riches in the book itself.

Introduction

Ayn Rand, born in St. Petersburg, Russia, in 1905, an ardent student imbued with Russian passion for western European culture (she learned to read French) experienced the glorious sunset of the Romantic Revolution. That movement, especially in literature, lasted longest (and arguably reached its heights) in France in the novels of Victor Hugo. Four of his five greatest were published in the 1860s and 1870s (the exception was the much earlier *Notre-Dame de Paris*), when Hugo was in his sixties.

They became Ayn Rand's lifelong inspiration along with a comparatively few other novels and plays by the last great Romanticists. When her own fiction achieved fame and a worldwide readership of millions, she used her platform to introduce new generations to Hugo. She told us that readers who had not experienced the profound optimism toward the future, the benevolence toward mankind—the sheer "gaiety"—in years prior to World War I, could never fully comprehend that sense of life. But they could glimpse it, share it for a time, in the novels of Hugo.

She viewed herself, she said later, as the "transmission belt" between that sunlit era and our own. And what she was transmitting was the spirit of Romantic literature, what she called, as a technical term, its "sense of life"—our deepest, most abiding, and influential emotions about existence, man's nature, his metaphysical "stature," and his place in the Universe.

The concept of "sense of life"

Sense-of-life emotions are our grand psychic summing-up of the meaning of our emotional responses to life. They are emotions so foundational to our outlook on life that they amount to an implicit metaphysics. Our sense of life is our stance toward the fact of existence, our psychological means of creating and experiencing art, and our lodestar in romantic love. In any given individual, a sense of life falls somewhere on the spectrum between the extremes of sheer malevolence and benevolence.

At the root of Romanticism, beneath its protean manifestations and diverse themes, is the premise of the individual's freedom of will: belief in man as a being of volitional consciousness. If man is genuinely free, his decisions and choices authentic, then his soul is his to fashion—in the end, to win or to lose. His choice of his values is an inescapable lifelong responsibility and challenge. To understand that his values are himself, what he has chosen to make of himself, is to understand why individuals may come into profound conflict—and self-conflict. Why history has seen heroes in epic battles, risking all, even life itself, for values they cherish.

In fiction, this can be grasped by a child. We all experience it. There's nothing like a great story of a hero "facing fearful odds" in a suspenseful struggle for what is "right." That is what Ayn Rand loved as a girl, encountered in Hugo and the Romantics as a young woman, and expended her prodigious talent to bring to readers of our era.

Heroes never disappeared from popular fiction or the hearts of readers; thrillers of every stripe are bestsellers year in and year out. Plot, suspense, protagonists of heroic stature, epic contests for justice, and the certainty that true love will prevail are the staples of "genre" fiction. (I look at this in the chapter, "What Is A Hero in Literature?") But they have disappeared from the realm of "literature," from novels that aspire to philosophical depth, psychological complexity, sophisticated characterization, and stylistic mastery.

By way of contrast, *Atlas Shrugged* has been praised—and damned—as relentlessly philosophical, with passages of explicit philosophy many pages long. It is a tribute to the vitality of Romanticism that at the same time it has been deemed "a philosophical thriller," "a philosophical detective story," a tour de force in "metaphysical humor," the "ultimate suspense novel," and a "literary mystery thriller."

The paradoxes of historical Romanticism

As I explain in this book's first chapter, the diversity of the themes that characterized the Romantic Revolution over some eight decades (1790 to 1870)—longer in some countries and some of the arts, such as music—seem on initial examination bewildering. A glorification of wild nature, a reverence for the age of knighthood and chivalry, a fascination with early death—to name a random three. How are these to be viewed as aspects of a unified "movement"? That is a question that I address at some length. Underlying the surface incoherence, we find at work the same radical affirmation of man's free will.

From the perspective of the mid-twentieth century, when the

schools of "Naturalism," then "Realism," had swept "serious" literature, Ayn Rand could look back on Romanticism and discern—as even Hugo did not in full—what truly constituted its spirit and power. What was essential and what accidental, what consistent with its vital spirit, and what contradictory.

This enabled her, as she progressed from novel to novel—and the growth that occurred from *We the Living* to *The Fountainhead* to *Atlas Shrugged* seems astounding—to attain a Romanticism of ruthless purity that with the writing of *Atlas Shrugged* endowed her art with unprecedented power. See the chapter, "Ayn Rand Resuscitates Dying Romanticism."

She had identified what gives Romanticism its incomparable ability to excite the imagination, lift the spirit, and inspire intense hero-worship. She mastered a literary method that rendered *Atlas Shrugged* and its events and heroes immortal in the minds of readers—part of an experience readers say no other fiction gave them—and made it literally life-changing. I give personal testimony to that experience in the chapter, "Incurable Atlas Fever."

What is "Romantic Realism"?

If in her novels she resuscitated the Romantic Revolution, she gave that movement at least a slender chance to grow against almost insurmountable cultural odds. She was able to do so by virtue of her parallel career as a philosopher. Even as her novels became more consciously, consistently Romantic, her own philosophy emerged and became more explicit, articulate, and complete. Her hope that the future might see a rebirth of Romanticism was heard by many of us.

In writing *Atlas Shrugged*, she was determined not only to create a grand epic of the clash of values on a world stage—at levels simultaneously intimately personal, social, political, and philosophical—but at the same time to define what *should* be a hero's values. If, in Romantic fiction, men and women embodied the grandeur of dedication to their values, what should those values be? As she put the assignment to herself: Define a philosophy for successfully living on earth.

Atlas Shrugged became perhaps the first Romantic novel in history with heroes who lived and acted not for conventionally accepted "highest values"—the prevailing conception of the noble—but by a philosophy and code of values identified by the author and introduced to the world in the pages of a novel. The rest is history, as a generation of mostly young readers turned the last page of *Atlas Shrugged* not only on fire to emulate its heroes but possessed of an explicit exposition of the ideas that made those heroes possible.

Later, Ayn Rand constructed within the framework of "Objectivism" (as she called her philosophy) a theory of esthetics, focused primarily on literature. Beginning with a definition of art—as "the selective recreation of reality according to the artist's metaphysical value judgments (that is, "sense of life")—she constructed a consistent philosophy of Romanticism, its role in human psychology, its relationship to morality, and how it has been virtually eradicated as a school of serious literature in our time.

Within this esthetic, set forth in *The Romantic Manifesto*, she located and named her own esthetic-literary innovation. "Romantic Realism," she wrote, aspires to project the grandeur of individuals fighting for values, but to go beyond that to portray values rationally appropriate to man, to living, to achieving happiness. This sharply distinguished Romantic Realism from, say, Sir Walter Scott's medieval romance, *Ivanhoe*, or Nathaniel Hawthorne's romance of early New England, *The Scarlet Letter*, or Victor Hugo's romance of the England of James II, *The Man Who Laughs* (which she deemed the greatest novel in world literature).

By making explicit (and inspiring) her case for the Romantic school of literature, with urgent personal importance as "emotional fuel" in the individual's life, and with a pivotal role in an individual's moral development, Ayn Rand intended to inspire and enable continuation of her revival of Romanticism. I look at some of the early developments in the chapter, "Who Are the New Romantic Novelists"?

Rediscovering Romantic masters

In the encroaching darkness of Russia after the Bolshevik Revolution of 1917, Ayn Rand gazed with desperate longing at American movies with their utterly unattainable glamour and zest for life. Later, in the United States, one of her earliest jobs was in a Hollywood script department. She never lost her passion for the movies and found a precious few to love and praise. Although literature was the overriding focus of her esthetics, her comments on cinema from the perspective of Romanticism's broad principles were perspicacious and arresting. She had no patience for Naturalism or Realism from Hollywood. I include here a single review of a film, "Cesare Mori: The Romantic Triumph as B-Grade Italian Cinema." It exemplifies the kind of Romantic treasures to be unearthed, occasionally, in movies from an earlier era.

Her special fondness for French Romanticism left Ayn Rand's admirers to make a few exciting discoveries of their own. Among mine have been the celebrated turn-of-the-century Polish novelist, Henryk Sienkiewicz (1846-1916), who, in a sense, was the true climax of the Romantic Revolution in literature. He came after and admired Victor Hugo, translating one of Hugo's last novels, *Ninety-Three*, into Polish. Sienkiewicz's own masterpiece, called in Poland "the Trilogy," is the literary equivalent almost of a Polish national anthem—keeping alive national aspirations and patriotism in the Polish people through an era of literally national extinction when Poland was ruthlessly ripped into sections that were absorbed into the Austrian, German, and Russian empires. For the "Trilogy" and other works, Sienkiewicz was awarded the Nobel Prize for Literature in 1905—simultaneously the first, only, and last Romantic novelist so honored. I introduce readers to the excitement and passion of Sienkiewicz in "Henryk Sienkiewicz and the Climax of Romanticism" and "The Great Romantic Novel You Never Have Read."

The Romanticist poets

Ayn Rand did not care much for poetry, although she had a few favorites among the Romanticists such as Rudyard Kipling and once characterized her novella, *Anthem*, as "poetry." My own literary passion, though, has been poetry, both as reader and writer, and I have identified, in the trends of poetry in our time, the same forces of philosophical incoherence and degradation that have affected all literature.

I argue, and the historical and logical case is unanswerable, that the defining characteristic of poetry is meter, the verse's underlying regular pattern of stressed and unstressed syllables. With deliberate, telling variations upon this underlying pattern, the poet achieves his only distinctively *poetic* effects. All the resources of prose are at work in poetry, as well, of course, but only meter distinguishes poetry from "poetical," "artful" prose.

Since about the 1940s, poets have deliberately dispensed with meter. Poetry that does not employ meter, of course, is "free verse." Presumably, it is "free" from the constraints of meter, enabling the liberated poet to say exactly what he means. Pity poor Shakespeare, Marlowe, Wordsworth, Byron, Shelley, Keats, Coleridge, Tennyson, Hardy, Yeats, Pound, Eliot—all of whom worked in the shackles of meter, presumably never "free" to say what they truly meant.

Two chapters, here, one on poetry's history, one on today's "free verse" racket, are tangentially relevant to Romanticism. The overarching issue is how the philosophy of Postmodernism, which today dominates universities, the professions, and the media, has infected all the arts. Reliably, *the Postmodernist assault in each case is directed at the essence of the art form: plot in fiction, pictorial representation in painting, meter in poetry, melody in music.*

Getting personal

I explore the origins of my own love affair with Romanticism in the essay "Tarzan and the Hero Within Us." I was six or seven, I think, when my father began bringing home used copies of the Tarzan books. Beginning, of course, with the immortal *Tarzan of the Apes*. We would sit side by side on the couch as he read to me. From the first, Edgar Rice Burroughs's soaring imagination and noble conception of man mesmerized me. I could not get enough of it. Living on a farm, woods adventures, animals in the wild, the challenge to the huntsman drew me almost daily.

The vision of the ceaselessly adventuring, unflinchingly bold warrior always on the side of the right—a hero to the good, terrifying to the evil—made a "moral sense of life" inseparable from my self-image and self-respect. Such a "sense" is not a code of morality, Ayn Rand has said, but a moral *stance* toward life, a mindset that values matter profoundly. Romantic fiction fosters exactly that in our early development. It was that force that dominated my journey into young manhood.

Other classic heroes of American and English literature, from Sherlock Holmes to Davy Crockett, joined my personal pantheon before the day that I picked up *Atlas Shrugged*. And Ayn Rand's heroes, of course, were not the last to which I thrilled in a lifetime of reading. But Ayn Rand's heroes became the ones that stepped from the pages of a book into my world. And it is they that I chose to emulate, in principle, for the next half-century—as I do today.

In this 2021 edition of *Romanticism Reborn*, I include a new chapter, "What Is Romanticism, Today?" My answer is narrower than my question. The subject of the essay is today's love affair with fantasy novels and films—perhaps the most widely read popular Romanticism. For new generations, fantasy is what detective and secret agent fiction were for earlier generations. That is a broad generalization, of course. The lesson, though, is that every generation, and individual, must find a way to experience the life-giving power of Romantic literature.

When "Realism" dominates so-called "serious" literature, the public will seek what it needs in popular Romanticism. It is no accident that *The Lord of the Rings*, the seminal work in the contemporary fantasy movement, is the best-selling novel of all time.

Walter Donway
East Hampton, June 2021

The Romantic Revolution: The Glory, the Paradoxes, the Future

This is from *Romanticism: A Very Short Introduction* by Michael Ferber (OUP Oxford, 2010):

"Since at least the 1920s, definitions of Romanticism have been sent aloft, shot down, repaired, relaunched, parodied, abandoned, rediscovered, and finally laid to rest, and revived from the dead through countless cycles of scholarship and journalism."

Ayn Rand identified her philosophy of literature as "Romanticism" and, in 1975, published a collection of essays that, together, she deemed *The Romantic Manifesto: A Theory of Literature*. The ideas in that book are among the most profound and persuasive in the history of the philosophy of esthetics. I would offer as just three examples: her discussion of 1) the practical value of art in man's life, 2) the nature and role of "sense of life" in creating and enjoying art, and 3) the epistemology of art in explaining why readers or listeners with the same sense of life prefer works of greater or lesser stylistic complexity based on the conceptual level upon which they characteristically operate.

The *Romantic Manifesto* is a masterful and inspiring exposition of those theories (and so much else). This essay is only indirectly about them. Instead, it is about:

- Why she chose to describe her literary esthetics as Romanticism
- Why so much Romantic literature, and the nature of the philosophy called Romanticism, makes her choice to identify herself with that school of art seem paradoxical or even incomprehensible
- In what sense she indeed does turn out to be a Romanticist

Addressing those questions might clarify a lot of historical confusion about Romanticism—but don't tell Michael Ferber. Then, we can look, all too briefly, at today's prospects for a new Romanticism in literature—a movement Ayn Rand hoped might be seeded by her publication of *The Romantic Manifesto*.

Romanticism

Ayn Rand identified herself, as a novelist, with one of the most dynamic thrusts in the history of the arts:

1) Romanticism was one of the most radical shifts from what came before it. That was, in a narrower artistic sense, Classicism—but, in a broader intellectual sense, the entire Enlightenment philosophy of reason, science, and this-worldliness. So, most literary historians and philosophers, such as British historian and philosopher, Isaiah Berlin, see Romanticism as quintessentially anti-Enlightenment. And make no mistake, the Romantic Movement is full of works of art, ideas, and explicit philosophies that are hostile not only to Classicism but to the Enlightenment and its most cherished premises and outlook. And that, of course, is one of the paradoxes for us, because Objectivism is NOT a rebellion against the fundamental premises of the Enlightenment. It is an Enlightenment philosophy. Should we qualify this with "except in esthetics"? That is one of our questions, today.

2) The Romantic Movement was one of the most popular—most democratic, if you will—movements in the history of art. It shattered the containment shell that had made classical art a pleasure and pursuit chiefly of the wealthy, "educated" upper class—the refined or leisure class. English poet George Gordon, Lord Byron's epic poetic narrative, "Child Harold's Pilgrimage," a landmark of Romanticism published first in 1812, sold 10,000 copies on its first day—an epic poem! And many decades later, long after the period historians identify as the Romantic Revolution, a million Frenchmen turned out for the funeral procession of the greatest Romantic novelist of all time, Victor Hugo. Between these two poles was a period in which a broad popular audience—the marketplace—replaced both aristocratic patronage and the endorsement of the classical "academies" as the path to an artist's success. And today, more than 150 years after the "end" of the Romantic Movement—usually put at 1850, at the latest—much of the best-selling, widely read fiction is the popular romanticism of thrillers, mysteries, literal "romances," fantasies, science fiction, and supernatural and horror stories.

3) The Romantic Movement was one of the most productive of great works that have sustained their critical reputation and popular appeal, decade after decade. Who are the British poets taught today in English-speaking schools around the world? What names come to

mind when we say "poet"? John Keats, Percy Shelley, William Taylor Coleridge, Lord Byron, William Blake, William Wordsworth—every one of them a Romanticist, though Blake, just from a chronological viewpoint, is a precursor of Romanticism. Yes, Classical poets like Alexander Pope, John Dryden, and Ben Jonson are studied; but not with the fervor brought to the Romanticists. I am not going to discuss the Romantic Movement in music, which produced works still virtually universal in the concert-hall repertoire, today. Nor am I going to discuss painting. Because, after all, Ayn Rand's subtitle of *The Romantic Manifesto* is "a theory of literature." She knew the value of defining context.

Ayn Rand chose the name of this movement for her literary esthetics and novels. We might have more insight into why she did this, had she discussed, and waxed enthusiastic about, more writers of the Romantic Movement. But she idolized—and called the greatest novelist in world literature—a writer in some respects idiosyncratic in the Romantic Movement. And she mentioned few others.

Victor Hugo as a "Romanticist"

Victor Hugo is deemed the greatest French novelist—also poet and perhaps playwright. True, some literary greats and critics, including some today, scoffed at that; but don't tell the French public. To a near approximation, Hugo is the only Romantic novelist that Ayn Rand discussed in any depth. It almost seems that she chose him to be *what she meant* by Romanticism in literature.

Yes, I know she called *The Scarlet Letter*, by Nathaniel Hawthorne, the greatest novel in American literature. And it is, unquestionably, the crown of the American Romantic Movement, but arrived late in that movement. And she brought Russian novelist Dostoyevsky into the fold by describing him as a "negative Romanticist." And those of us who bought everything sold by the old NBI Book Service could mention, *Quo Vadis*, by Henryk Sienkiewicz, a wonderful novel published in Polish in 1895. Sienkiewicz was awarded the Nobel Prize in Literature in 1905, perhaps the only Nobel Prize awarded to a Romantic novelist.

Ayn Rand's almost exclusive focus on Hugo raises questions. Hugo made his reputation as a poet and playwright early in his life. But he published four of his five great novels in the 1860s and early 1870s (when Hugo, by the way, was in his 60's). This was well after the end of the Romantic Revolution in literature. *The Man Who Laughs*, which 'no one" has read, was published in 1869 and Ayn Rand calls it "the greatest novel in world literature." Some of you may recall that in her essay, "The *Comprachicos*," she began with a scene from that novel, a profoundly religious scene, but generically a tribute to the nobility of human morality—and called it one of the greatest scenes in world literature.

Let me summarize. The sole example of Romanticism in literature to which Ayn Rand paid any real attention was a French Romanticist who wrote during the twilight of world literary Romanticism. But the Romantic Revolution, if chronology means anything—and if imitation by later writers around Europe and America means anything—was launched and largely defined by German philosophers and artists. What is more, Victor Hugo wrote his novels well into the rise of Naturalism—the literary school Ayn Rand contrasted with Romanticism and considered her esthetic opponent. In other words, she appears to concentrate on a narrow and idiosyncratic slice of the long, varied, and emphatically multi-national Romantic Movement in literature—and then identifies herself with that movement.

I do not intend to be contrary. I am trying to capture for you the paradoxes raised by her choice of "Romanticism" as a name for her literary esthetics. And, yes, I think I am trying to convey my initial sense of confusion as I became familiar with the Romantic Movement as a whole—and sought to relate it to Ayn Rand.

Objectivism and Romanticism: the Paradoxes

These, then, are **two paradoxes** we face in understanding how to reconcile the historical Romantic Revolution with Ayn Rand's choice of that label.

The first paradox is that historians, I think with few exceptions, view the Romantic Revolution—some say, the "Romantic Rebellion"— as a rejection not only of Classicism but of the premises of the Enlightenment: reason, science, a this-worldly perspective, and a metaphysical lightness (a relief at rejecting religion, superstition, and Medievalism). And this rejection of the Enlightenment, as I said, was real—except that it did tend to characterize German Romanticism more than it did British Romanticism and certainly French Romanticism. Nevertheless, some rejection of the Enlightenment is a defining characteristic of Romanticism in every nation and throughout the period. German Romanticism is identified with German Idealism—the philosophy of Immanuel Kant, Johann Gottlieb Fichte, the brothers Schlegel, and, latterly, Georg Wilhelm Friedrich Hegel. I will remind you that this is the philosophical movement—the German gang—that Ayn Rand identifies as assaulting the Enlightenment and poisoning the roots of contemporary philosophy and culture. So that is paradox number one. The Romantic Movement was a rebellion against the Enlightenment.

The second paradox requires no examination of premises on the fundamental philosophical level. It arises from surveying Romantic literature of every nation and era—except perhaps France in the twilight of the Romantic Movement—to identify its themes. In every country, every segment of the 70-plus-year Romantic Movement, the most identifiable themes of literature are these:

The awe of nature. Romanticism brought a religious passion to the concept of Nature unsullied by the Industrial Revolution, urbanization, science. The Romanticists—I am thinking, now, of the British poets—Blake, Wordsworth, Keats, Shelley, Coleridge—went in awe of "unspoiled" nature's beauty, power, and splendor. Perhaps the most influential and characteristically American philosophical and artistic movement was Transcendentalism, the philosophy of Ralph Waldo Emerson and Henry David Thoreau—and earlier implicit in the work of James Fenimore Cooper—later, in the work of poet Emily Dickinson. Here, the pantheism of the Romantic Movement, the identification of God with nature, became frank and explicit.

The mythic, the folkloric. The Romanticists in all countries turned for their inspiration to folklore and myth, usually of their region. This was the beginning of German Romanticism, certainly, and spread rapidly. These were not the formalized myths of the Classicists from Greek and Roman mythology, but the old tales, folk legends, folk heroes, and superstitions and mysteries from the Romanticists backyard. The German Romanticists elevated this into virtual worship of the German past, German folk, and German sensibility, as such. But an enterprising Scottish writer brought out tales of alleged Irish and Scottish mythical heroes called the "Ossian" cycle that had an incalculable impact on British and French Romanticism. (The Germans had become persuaded that their mythology had to be their own and could be properly understood only by themselves. But they granted it was the same in each country.)

The superiority of the historic, especially the Medieval. The Scottish poet and novelist, Sir Walter Scott, became the first internationally celebrated British writer in modern times, writing novel after novel that not only became hugely popular but made the art of the novel itself respectable. The *Waverly* novels, *Ivanhoe*, *Rob Roy*, and a bookshelf of others all were historic. The earlier ones were set in the Scottish Borders where outlaws and fierce clan chieftains and heroes of the resistance to the English all were a bit mixed together. In *Ivanhoe*, Scott turned to Medieval times, the period of Norman hegemony over the Saxons in England. This is considered his masterpiece, a hugely popular novel, and an example of hundreds of works of the Romantic period that glorified the Medieval period as a nobler, more inspiring, more heroic era than the industrial and commercial revolution then underway. English writer John Ruskin made this theme into an explicit and extremely influential credo.

The glorification of early death—especially of poets and tragic lovers. (Are you getting a sense of the consistency of these themes with Objectivism? I didn't think so.) Byron, the acknowledged hero of British Romantic poetry, went to join the war for Greek independence and died there, at 37, of fever. The glory of his sacrifice, and the many paintings of his handsome physique in death, continued and accelerated a powerful Romantic theme of the glory and beauty of early death. The young Wolfgang Goethe, in his 20's, published *The Sorrows of Young Werther*, about the suicide of a jilted young lover (who, in his sorrow, read aloud from the Ossian stories, by the way). *Werther* is said to have inspired an entire youth movement, "*Sturm and Drang*," in Germany—part and parcel of German Romanticism. It has become a shibboleth that the novel inspired suicides all over Germany, but historians admonish that there is no documentation.

There are many other themes of the Romantic Movement in literature, such as the deification of the poet as creator, fascination with the supernatural, and horror.

The Enlightenment and three revolutions

But I should move on, now, to start addressing the questions I have raised. Since we are talking, here, about historic causation—how the ideas of one movement, the Enlightenment, fared in a later movement, Romanticism—let us look at the timelines.

The Enlightenment, of course, cannot be said to have started in a given year, or even a given decade, but let us say it was stirring by 1650 and took off by 1700. Over the century following that, the Enlightenment is said to have led to three major revolutions:

- **Industrial Revolution**, which is not easy to pinpoint historically, but really "takes off" by 1750.
- **Political revolution**, including the American Revolution of 1776 and the French Revolution of 1789 and after.
- **The Romantic Revolution**, which we can say was a recognized, European-wide movement by 1800.

I use the term "*led to*," by the way, not "*caused*," because so many historians see the Romantic Revolution, or Rebellion, as caused by the Enlightenment only in the sense of being a reaction against it.

The timeline is clear: The Enlightenment achieves full power in 1700; 50 years later, the Industrial Revolution really kicks in; 25 years after that, the American and French Revolutions occur; and 25 years after that, the Romantic Revolution is underway. A busy and glorious century.

One thing to notice is that Ayn Rand, the quintessential Enlightenment philosopher, embraces **all three of these revolutions** of unprecedented power: one that liberated man from slavery to the natural world; one that liberated man from his fellow man in the political field; and one...

...that what? What is the Romantic Revolution doing in this list— and in Objectivism? As I have said, repeatedly, literary historians and philosophers characterize Romanticism not as a revolution extending the Enlightenment, but as a counter-revolution against the Enlightenment, a rebellion against Enlightenment premises.

Well, you point to Germany and what you see makes that hard to refute, but I would suggest to you that Germany was not a country of the Enlightenment—not in the full sense we see in Britain, France, and America. Religion did not get anything like the same skeptical scrutiny in Germany. There was no political revolution toward liberty in Germany. Nor did the Industrial Revolution take hold in Germany in the same way as in Britain and America. Germany, at this time, was not a nation but a group of independent states, most of them ruled by despots who suppressed new ideas, and very much under the heel of France. What we do see, in the state of Prussia, is the beginnings of the systematic philosophical destruction of the Enlightenment, to be replaced by the German idealism of Kant and a long line of his powerful successors. (Kant did not embrace the Romantic Revolution, by the way, just as he did not embrace—not openly—an attack on the Enlightenment. Kant, along with Leibniz and Goethe, are considered the core German Enlightenment philosophers. (A theme of the German Enlightenment was combining reason and religion.)

One of Isaiah Berlin's chief theses is that what happened in Germany was a rebellion against the French Enlightenment out of envy and resentment at the conqueror (France)—and that rebellion took the form of the earliest Romanticism. But all this was a dynamic distinctive to Germany.

In England, Scotland, and France, the Romanticists *did* think they were liberating man, liberating man's spirit from what they saw as the constraints and conformity of the Enlightenment. But they were not opposed to reason and most of them were devotees of science. Most were ardent supporters of the American Revolution. Many were fierce advocates of the French Revolution, at the outset, and made extravagant statements that came back to mortify them when the French Revolution became The Terror.

To pursue the contrast with Germany, let me say that Isaiah Berlin argues that even the French philosopher Jean Jacques Rousseau was not anti-Enlightenment because he did believe that reason can identify how man should live. Berlin argues that in his tone and rhetoric Rousseau sounded more like a Romanticist than an Enlightenment man. And Rousseau did publish the best-selling novel of the 18th Century, *Julie, or the New Heloise*. But this was in 1754, half a century before the Romantic Revolution. He is best seen as a transition from the Enlightenment to Romanticism.

The "Sensibility" movement" as transition

If you can hold in mind this framework of explanation, then I can insert a footnote or qualifier. Historians today find it easier to explain what happened between the reign of Classicism and the reign of Romanticism by postulating an intermediate period. The name they give it is the "Sensibility" movement. Think of Classicism with its emphasis on reason, ideal forms, order, a calmly thoughtful approach to all things. And then, think of the Sensibility movement as tapping the Enlightenment on the shoulder and saying, "I applaud all you are doing, but, don't forget, human beings have emotions, passions—and in explaining and understanding the human condition it often is feeling—or feeling in conflict with reason—or passion—or irrationality—that is foremost. Just wanted to remind you."

And the Sensibility movement runs from perhaps 1760 to 1800. A defining work is *The Sorrows of Young Werther,* by Goethe. The style and tone of Rousseau, and his novel, *Julie*, are of this period.

Continuing this line of explanation, Romanticism arrives on the scene and exaggerates and exalts Sensibility, but, above all, it criticizes it for viewing emotional man as passive, reactive—not as the active valuer, the master of his destiny, that became the Romantic hero. Positing this movement called "Sensibility" makes the change from Classicism to Romanticism more understandable and realistic.

Romanticism as the third movement for liberation

The Romanticists saw themselves liberating man's spiritual, emotional, and artistic nature. They were liberating his individuality, his nature as a being characterized not only by reason, but feeling and choice, by a sense of power over his world, by imagination, by a sense of himself as heroic.

Romanticists sought liberation from the Enlightenment's singular emphasis on reason, science, and the conquest of the material world by the Industrial Revolution. They saw man's life, with the demise of religion, as impoverished by lacking a sense of awe at his place in the Universe: his ability to stand on the mountaintop—or a great rock over the crashing waves—and glory in his metaphysical stature on Earth.

The Romanticists looked around themselves for the "more." As they turned from the strict Enlightenment spirit, they became fascinated with nature *not* tamed by science, *not* tamed by industrial development; they became fascinated with life's deep fears and tragedies, such as early death, to which logic and science seemed to be only neutral; they became enchanted with the supernatural (not so much the religious variety) and sometimes with horror; they all looked back in history to see if anything mankind once had, had been lost—and thought they found it in heroic deeds of the past, great individual heroes, love beyond the bounds of calculation and propriety.

But was this a rebellion against foundational premises of the Enlightenment? Or was there here, too, an extension of the Enlightenment—another essential *liberation* stemming from the Enlightenment? A liberation of the spirit to be equated with the revolutions in man's material existence and political freedom? I believe there was such a liberation.

The Enlightenment had become entranced with the power of principles, theories, and laws; it gloried in them, as well it might. Science was explaining the whole of material existence—Earth and its place in the heavens—and it all made amazing sense. In all fields, the power of generalizations, principles, was explored. In the American Revolution, the principles of man's rights, proper government, and delegation and limitation of political power were applied to the everlasting benefit of mankind. The Enlightenment sought principles everywhere: types, ideal types—and, always, the right way, the rules, for doing anything.

Understandably, then, the initial esthetic of the Enlightenment was Classicism, the belief that the principles of beauty, order, proportion, and restraint had been perfected in Ancient Greek, and, particularly, Roman art. That esthetic had been a life-giving breakout into freedom during the early Renaissance when European civilization discovered the sublime portrayal of man and nature in the Classical world. After centuries of art devoted singularly to religious themes—magnificent, imaginative art, but all on one endlessly varied note—turning to the affirmation of human beauty, nobility, and worldliness in ancient art was pure light.

Then, during the Enlightenment, a whole new, unlimited world had been discovered. And yet, the dozens of official academies across Europe would look only backward to Greece and Rome. There were rules for all acceptable art. Classicism was fixated on "ideal types." More than 100 academies, at one point, were defining, teaching, and righteously defending the proper principles of art. It was Howard Roark's neo-Classical dean become Dr. Frankenstein's monster. The academies guarded the public against any work not deemed to conform to"right" reason, the rules.

Romanticism retorts to Enlightenment" Classicism

The Romanticists retorted—resoundingly, and for decades—that all truth in art arises within the individual. What rules should an artist follow in choosing the subject matter and theme of a poem, a novel, a painting, or a sonata? You may recognize the following famous reply by a Romanticist: "Art is the selective recreation of reality according to the artist's metaphysical value judgments."

What is Ayn Rand saying? That the mind of every human being integrates its emotional responses over a whole lifetime, integrates them automatically into a grand sum that represents an implicit judgment on the world and the human condition. This sum has the weight of an implicit metaphysics; it functions as a subconscious fundamental outlook on the world, a feeling for what is or is not "right"—but using "right" in the sense of fitting into a worldview. And this most powerful emotional sum, this judgment on life itself, guides the artist in creating his world, the homeland of his soul, in his art. "Sense of life," as Ayn Rand called it, is the fountainhead of creativity in art and enables us to enjoy art. The artist's only disastrous failure is to create not from his sense of life but some imitation of "good art," some concept of "the right kind of art." The only futile journey of the artist is one that does not begin and end in the homeland of his own soul.

You see how radically that view of the nature of art, the artist, and the response to art differs from the esthetic of Classicism. By the nature of art, not everyone will enjoy a given artist's work as everyone will, or should, accept a scientist's valid demonstration of scientific truth. Some will find an artist's sense of life inimical to all they feel—ugly, a lie. Others will cry, "Yes!" In art, their "truth" is a recognition of the reality of the homeland of their soul.

It is easy to see, looking at Germany during the Romantic Revolution, how easily this valid insight into art can be associated with a disastrous philosophy, a philosophy proclaiming the individual perceives his own reality—and that reality is "true for him." I oversimplify Idealism, of course, but German Romantic philosophy is shot through with this theme. It became a dogma about a truth to which the German folk, the German nation, the German race were privy. Thus, Isaiah Berlin views German Romanticism as the philosophic prelude to the calamity of 20th Century Germany.

Romanticism in art as genuine individualism

But Romanticism as manifested in art, and *limited* to art, is an assertion of individualism, choice, and valuing. Art deals with values— our deepest value judgments:the ones that shape our soul—a perdurable outlook on the world with hope, or despair, or tragic resignation, or courageous opposition; our feeling for mankind; our confidence or lack of confidence in human metaphysical freedom.

Ayn Rand does not see the role of art as to change those metaphysical values; that is the job of philosophy. Art's role and value is to give the individual the experience of the reality of his metaphysical values, of experiencing what it would be like to live in the homeland of his soul.

Morality's role is to define, by reason, the values appropriate for man to pursue, given his nature and the nature of reality. Morality is about objectivity, seeing things as they are and defining how to survive over his whole life span and at the level we call "flourishing," which brings emotions of happiness.

In contrast to morality, art is about whatever metaphysical value judgments we have reached. Art is about how to enjoy, during some moments of life, the reality of our metaphysical values—and to gain from that experience the motivation, which Ayn Rand called "emotional fuel," to go on. The affirmation of the individual soul—and its metaphysical glory because it chooses its values—is Romanticism.

And that is why, for all its follies—its colorful quest for inspiration in haunted castles, pirates on the high seas, knights jousting in days of yore, outlaws of the Scottish border, and star-crossed lovers—Romantic art is a product of the Enlightenment. In art, the role of reason is to start with the fundamental reality of human volition and then motivate us to embrace and fight for values, to put man the value-worshiper at the center of his universe, to glorify man as a being of self-made soul.

And this, of course, is what Ayn Rand loved in the novels of Victor Hugo: the stature of men when fighting for values as such. But we also find in Hugo many subordinate themes of Romanticism. In *Toilers of the Sea,* there is the awesome power of the untamed natural world, the sea—and the man who pits himself against it, for love. In *The Man Who Laughs,* we have nature at its most awesome, a historical theme, a full-blown royal court, exotic characters of another age and two individuals—one hideously deformed, one exquisitely beautiful but blind—who fall in love almost as though in a scientifically controlled experiment in pure love for another soul.

In every Hugo novel, as Ayn Rand shows us, there is the grandeur inherent in the metaphysical freedom of man to choose his values. Man is the species that falls in love with values and can know love based on shared values. And the species that needs, psychologically, as the fuel for the courage to work for his values, to experience vicariously their reality in a world created by art.

Grasping the triad of liberating revolutions

The Romantic Movement completed the triad of liberating revolutions that owe their origin to the philosophy of the Enlightenment. The Industrial Revolution freed man from the subhuman animal's subjection to nature; it made his values the force shaping that material world. The Political Revolution freed man from subjection to other men; it left his values free to shape his own life and happiness. The Romantic Revolution freed man's spirit from subjection to the dogma that in art there is one intrinsically right sense of life; it left him free to create and enjoy art arising from his own deepest sense-of-life emotions.

Immediately after publication of *Atlas Shrugged*, acolytes of Ayn Rand set about formulating Ayn Rand's fiction into a new classicism—and many still strive to do so. Movies were recommended to me with the remark, "It will be good for your sense of life." Although Ayn Rand gave a course on fiction writing to inner-circle students, they and other Objectivists wrote little fiction while Ayn Rand was alive. The new "classicism" set standards too fearfully high.

To me, it is a dramatic demonstration of Ayn Rand's ability and willingness to look at things simply as they are that she realized that esthetics cannot formulate some "right" sense of life for the artist or audience. Esthetics, unlike ethics, cannot be prescriptive of subject matter. The novel as an artwork is not concerned with instilling values but with nourishing a value-centric perspective on life. It is the branch of philosophy that, more than any other, considers the individual human being's needs—here, now, as he is. And that was the lodestar of the Romantic Revolution.

Nothing better characterizes Romanticism than that it was the revolution that invited every individual to life's party.

Historians scoff at the possibility of defining Romanticism, maintaining that its elements are so diverse that no definition can integrate them. Perhaps, but I am going to summarize, here, by offering some definitions:

Romanticism is a philosophy of esthetics maintaining that art should express and assert the artist's actively chosen values and deepest emotions, including the irrational and fanciful, recreating the world in the image of those values.

Romanticism rejects the Naturalist view of art's role as to portray the world the artist sees and experiences around him. It rejects the esthetic of Classicism that art should embody a timeless ideal of beauty based upon principles discoverable by studying the art of the past.

Romantic Realism, the name Ayn Rand gave her approach to literature, modifies generic Romanticism by adding that a given artist may choose to identify rational values and a reasoned perspective on the world for his heroes and thus project in fiction a morality for achieving happiness.

Romanticism today

Introducing *The Romantic Manifesto*, Ayn Rand denied it was the manifesto of an existing movement; there was no Romantic movement, but she hoped her book might help to give birth to one. That was over 50 years ago. Look at our timeline from the Enlightenment to its three revolutions. Fifty years is long enough for a major movement to arise—perhaps not to peak, but certainly to be in evidence.

But no widely known artists identify themselves as Romanticists. There are no widely disseminated philosophical statements advocating Romanticism. No "school" anywhere of Romanticists banded together. No best-selling novels that any critics have identified as Romanticist. And, most of all: there is *no opposition* to such a movement, no attempt to quash it, ridicule it, undercut it. You may be sure that if inroads were being made on today's prevailing schools of naturalist-realist literature, and gaining ground, the intruder would be attacked mercilessly. As Ayn Rand was attacked, and the original Romanticists were attacked by the Classicists.

Romanticism in popular fiction

Ayn Rand wrote a great deal about the unquenchable popularity of Romanticism and noted that modern "popular" fiction—not literature, not works considered "serious"—was the almost exclusive domain—I think she said, the last holdout—of Romanticism. Agatha Christie and Mickey Spillane hugely popularized the detective novel, with a clearly delineated battle between good and evil, a conflict of values pared down to crime and criminal justice. Ian Fleming launched a seemingly unstoppable avalanche of spy and secret agent thrillers. Ayn Rand loved these authors and made them required reading among Objectivists. And at *this* level, yes, Romanticism was attacked, ridiculed, satirized, and undercut—as she indicated in her essay, "Bootleg Romanticism." It was far too successful for the comfort of the establishment critics.

But nothing could stop it and, today, I sometimes wonder if the sheer number of new mysteries and thrillers coming onto the market will provide each reader with a novel uniquely his own. One author, one reader. The top writers in this category—I would mention Ken Follett and Frederick Forsyth and the early John LeCarre—are far more imaginative, powerful, and better craftsmen than most writers considered "serious."

Nevertheless, all write to formulas, however imaginatively elaborated, all deal with values mostly in terms of crime and punishment or good agents versus malefactors. That is not the nature of literature; compare *The Fountainhead* with any of these mysteries and thrillers. Compare how long you can contemplate the meaning of the value conflicts, characters, and ideas in *The Fountainhead* as compared with the magnificent thriller, *The Jackal,* which I have re-read three times without once thinking anything. And it is not because *The Fountainhead* is a "novel of ideas." The same comparison can be made between *The Scarlet Letter* and Agatha Christie's best. Or *Les Miserables*, *Frankenstein* (the complete title is *Frankenstein or The Modern Prometheus*), *Pride and Prejudice* and your favorite thriller or mystery.

That I know of no contemporary Romantic literature apart from the novels of Ayn Rand does not mean new Romantic novelists aren't out there. But they are relatively invisible and major artistic movements, by definition, are visible.

The Romantic Manifesto and the novels of Ayn Rand inspired novelists of a new generation of novelists. Mark Tier, who writes fiction, recently compiled a list of 30 first novels that were inspired by Ayn Rand. The list is available on Amazon in the form of the actual novels for sale—with cover, blurb, and author profile, plus access to that writer's other novels. Its earliest entries are from decades ago—Ayn Rand's associates, Kay Nolte Smith and Ericka Holzer. Oddly, it includes *King Rat*, a novel of Japanese prisoner of war camp survival by James Clavell, the famous author of *Shogun,* who admired Ayn Rand's works.

But the great majority of novels on the list are more recent, written by Objectivists who published their work "indie." The means published without convincing a literary agent or publisher—or anyone—that the novel is worth publishing. Not many of these novels have been noticed, though one exception is *Hunter*, by Robert Bidinotto, a first novel by a lifelong professional writer. It has sold well and has fans awaiting Robert's next. It is a fine novel, but one following the formula of battle between criminals and agents of justice—in this case, with a vigilante twist.

A couple of novels in the list of 30 that I have read depart from the mystery or secret-agent formula. *The Frankenstein Candidate*, by Vinay Kolhatkar, is about a modern political election and an ideal candidate; *Cossacks in Paris*, by Jeff Perren, is rather "classical" Romanticism, to mix my terms. An Enlightenment-era engineer, who talks much like Thomas Jefferson, is drafted into Napoleon's army, about to invade Russia. Both are "indie," with their authors the only ones to promote them, with no advertising budget, no bookstore sales—but with the potential of the gigantic Amazon machine.

I wish I had read more on this list of 30, and I will.

What is a new Romantic Movement waiting for? I would remind you that the Romantic Movement that emerged in 1800 was one of three revolutions that, I have argued, were inspired by the Enlightenment—the dominant philosophy of the century before. And then, I would ask: Do we have the underlying philosophical foundation, today—I mean not just the ideas but their predominance in our culture—to launch an American Revolution? Do we have the foundation to launch a new Industrial

Revolution?

Then why would we think ourselves ready to launch a Romantic Revolution?

I leave you with that thought. And with some lines written by the last and greatest Romantic poet, William Butler Yeats, in the wake of World War I, which Ayn Rand and so many others have said separates our world by an almost unbridgeable spiritual distance from the world born of the Enlightenment—including the Romantic Movement.

Yeats wrote, in 1919, in the aftermath of WWI:

> "Many ingenious lovely things are gone That
> seemed sheer miracle to the multitude..."

Atlas Shrugged Resuscitates Dying Romanticism

"It was a concerto of immense deliverance…" *--Atlas Shrugged*

The quotation is from *Atlas Shrugged*, characterizing the music of the composer, Richard Halley, a character undoubtedly in the image of the great musicians of the Romantic era. Tchaikovsky and Rachmaninoff come to mind.

To me, though, it applies supremely well to *Atlas Shrugged* itself and what it meant to individual readers like me, potentially to Ayn Rand's adopted homeland, perhaps to mankind's future…

Ayn Rand delivered the novel from the stranglehold of "Realism," which she called "Naturalism," by resuscitating its opposite—the school of Romanticism—after its near-death experience at the end of the nineteenth century.

If art—as she said—"builds the model" defined by an ethics, giving us the inspiration of encountering the ideal man,

And if art is the way a mind can be awakened to the world of moral values—and sustained by the emotional fuel that art provides,

Then, this was the "deliverance" most deeply personal to the individual.

Let me make that even more personal. For me, the one overwhelming experience of Objectivism was reading *Atlas Shrugged* and, at that moment, coming to love Dagny, Hank, Francisco, John… Just that personal is the experience of art.

I urge you to consider, today, that Ayn Rand's resuscitation of a Romantic Movement that to all appearances had decayed from its philosophical roots upwards was among her most original achievements.

She did at least three needful things:

1. She grasped the singular role of art, but particularly Romantic art, in human consciousness. In her teenage years, Romantic art was still a contemporary reality—at least in French literature and in music; she devoted her career to writing a Romantic novel so great that no cultural killers could strangle it in the crib. Like the infant Hercules, *Atlas* reached out to seize the attacking serpents by their necks and has never let go.

2. She worked out a philosophy of art, of esthetics, integrated into the structure of an entire philosophy of reason, egoism, and individualism.

She worked out the relationship of Romantic art to metaphysics, epistemology, and ethics. And then, she explained how her theory was psychologically actualized in the achievement of art's effects—including a child's development of a moral sense of life.

3. Not least, like her idol, Victor Hugo, she wrote essays about the glory of art, its sacred role in man's soul, and specific works and artists—and did so in astonishingly colorful, logically compelling essays. Readers who never had thought about esthetics, art's role in a culture, and art's decisive impact on human development and motivation, sat up, frowned, and took notice. These were life-and-death matters for each soul, for any culture.

To harken back to my statement a bit earlier: My thesis is that resuscitation of Romanticism—in the form of Romantic Realism—was Ayn Rand's *single most original philosophical achievement*. But, after all, why get into that irresolvable quibble? What was God's greatest achievement? That He created the female human breast? Or that he knew a good thing when he saw it and made two of them?

In most of her philosophy, Ayn Rand is not a fount of "new" philosophical ideas, what we label "originality."

How could she be? She searched for human greatness and had the honesty to herald it wherever she found it: Aristotle, St. Thomas Aquinas, John Locke, Thomas Jefferson: in arguments against God's existence, David Hume; Adam Smith and some of the French *philosophes*; and then, Ludwig von Mises and the Austrian School; and, in thought about how political structures free man's productive energy, Isabel Patterson and Herbert Spencer; in Romanticism, the great tradition culminated with Victor Hugo.

The fashion of twentieth-century philosophy has been scorched-earth "originality." All philosophy before my new school has been deluded. Metaphysics is mere myth; only linguistic analysis is truly "doing philosophy." No abstract principles are valid; the truth of an idea is its practice, its pragmatic results. Truth is not any given idea; it is your existential commitment to an idea, any idea, especially if it makes you nauseous. Or to go back further, to Kant: look in the mind to discover what is "out there." Or Karl Marx, whose originality liberated him from the insights of the entire tradition of classical economics. Scorched earth.

Ayn Rand's achievement was to identify, by rigorous standards, the best in the Western tradition since Aristotle, ruthlessly select the essential, integrate it with a brilliance that multiplied its value, apply it to more contemporary issues than perhaps any contemporary philosopher, and present it to a new generation in her fiction and nonfiction.

We know what she viewed as the challenges to the Western tradition, challenges she must overcome:

- The Kantian school's mission to re-infect the Enlightenment with faith disguised as reason.
- The devastating contradiction of faith and altruism with the requirements of man's life on Earth and with capitalism.
- The vulnerability of the conceptual level of knowledge to attack from subjectivism.
- The so-called "is-ought problem."

Ayn Rand had a penetrating appreciation of what the civilization the Western tradition had made possible and exposed its malicious enemies and their game. She told new generations in America—that's us, here—that the historically unimaginable life that we took for granted, today, was made possible by those ideas—those intellectual heroes—and that we were under deadly assault, all that we cherished at risk. That the enemies of man and life on this Earth had not vanished, only disguised their aim and bided their time; and, she cried: "Don't let it go…"

In discussing this with my brother, Roger Donway, he offered, as usual, an ironclad summary: "[S]he was the greatest modern voice of the Aristotelian tradition, updating it to take account of Enlightenment political liberty and the productive virtues of the Industrial Revolution."

The resuscitation of the Romantic Movement

The thrust of my presentation, today, can be captured by the addition of one clause to that summary: "and to take account of the exaltation of the human spirit made possible by the Romantic Revolution."

If Ayn Rand had been an associate professor at a liberal arts college—say, Kenyon, since Ohio had a special meaning for her—and preached the value of the Western tradition—would we have heard of her? Her colleagues would have patted her on the head and smirked. Yes, yes, everyone acknowledges the richness of the Western tradition.

But Ayn Rand understood how human beings become conscious moral agents, attentive to right and wrong—by whatever moral standard.

How they attach to their moral convictions the feeling: "this is the best within me." Our heroes instruct our souls, so that Jesus—or John Galt—becomes for us the image of our best aspirations. A hero, in simplest terms, is the embodiment of a moral ideal. A hero is a morality, and, more broadly, philosophy, up and walking. In answering the question: "What is the goal of your writing [in this case, novels]?" Ayn Rand answered: "To create the ideal man."

Without this achievement, as she implies in discussing the role of art in projecting a moral ideal (in *The Romantic Manifesto*), her philosophy could not have prevailed against the almost total embargo by the academic world and mainstream establishment. But let me add immediately that she did not view art merely as a great way to get across ideas opposed by the culture. She writes that art is *indispensable* in conveying *any* moral philosophy; it is the *only* way. Here is the relevant passage:

"When we come…to the task of defining moral principles and projecting what man ought to be…the results are almost impossible to communicate without the assistance of art. An exhaustive treatise will not do it…will not convey what an ideal man would be like and how he would act: no mind can deal with so immense a sum of abstraction…. There is no way to integrate such a sum without projecting an actual human figure…

"Hence the sterile, uninspiring futility of a great many theoretical discussions of ethics…Art is the indispensable medium for the communication of a moral ideal…"

By the way, as sometimes happens with Ayn Rand, we have slipped in just two paragraphs from "*almost* impossible" to "indispensable…" but the point is well made. On this account, she had no choice but to write novels if she wished to launch her philosophy in the world. Unless, of course, she wrote her philosophical treatises and hoped an admirer would come along someday and write the novels. That has been the case with most philosophers. If Jesus was the philosopher, then his apostles and others were the "novelists" writing in the *Bible* the story of the moral hero who changed all human history.

Ayn Rand's unique achievement was to identify Romanticism, but particularly the Romantic novel, as the greatest vehicle ever created to "project an actual human figure"—to "project" such a figure, not to "describe it" as in Naturalism or Realism. And then, to realize that to make Romanticism the means of projecting a figure based upon a philosophy, especially an ethics, for living successfully in the world, her heroes must walk through the world we live in now. To do that, she *reconnected* a moribund traditional Romanticism with its roots in the Enlightenment. She eliminated or downplayed elements of Romanticism inconsistent with Enlightenment reason. And so created what she called "Romantic Realism."

In the previous chapter, I argued that the historical Romantic Movement (which is dated from 1775 to 1850) had many non-Enlightenment (and non-Objectivist) themes. A few of them were an emphasis on will as against reason, intuition over intellect, heroic action over cogitation, fascination with horror and evil, noble sacrifices and beautiful deaths, and, above all, *obsession with the past.* But, I argued, Romanticism nevertheless was one of three great revolutions deriving from the Enlightenment. Those revolutions were political (e.g., the American and French revolutions), industrial, and artistic.

For all its non-Enlightenment baggage—a great deal of it originating in German philosophy—Romanticism was the legitimate offspring of the Enlightenment. That is because Romanticism's essence and motor were the supremacy—and glory—of the individual's freely judging and valuing mind. That was and is its core, whatever its other baggage.

For Romanticists themselves, by the way, the sharpest *conscious* contrast at the time was to Classicism. Classicism was the pervasive, powerful, and in the end, dogmatic movement that preceded Romanticism. Classicism arose not from the Enlightenment but the Renaissance and insisted that art ideally should follow known, intrinsically correct, universal rules defined by ancient Greek and Roman artists. Artists competed to express a kind of Platonic ideal of the Classical. Classicism, though gloriously life-giving and beautiful in its revival of the glory that was Greece and the grandeur that was Rome, tended to harden, over the centuries, into the mindset of Howard Roark's dean at his school of architecture.

The achievements of the Romantic era hardly can be overstated. It produced the greatest poetry ever written in English: Keats, Shelley, Byron, Blake, Wordsworth, and Coleridge.... The first worldwide "best-selling novels," such as Sir Walter Scott's *Ivanhoe.* Painters we still consider giants in our cultural history. And musical compositions that audiences never stop demanding and loving, no matter how hard impresarios of "modern music" push the "new," "original," and "cutting edge."

But, all the great Romantic novelists (and the novel is our focus, here, *The Romantic Manifesto* is subtitled, "A Philosophy of Literature," not of art) were infected by the non-Enlightenment features of Romanticism. Chief among these was an obsession with a better, happier, nobler past.

The Romantic mentality: Lost in the "glorious" past

I am going to focus, here, on the near-universal tendency of Romanticists to set their novels in an idealized and glorified past. Let this symbolize, for us, the much wider tendency to view the present time—that meant, especially in England, the Industrial Revolution—as just not... Romantic. The past was viewed through a golden haze of nostalgia as a time of lost glory. Thus, Victor Hugo set *The Man Who Laughs*, which Rand called "the greatest novel in world literature," in the era of fearsome King James II, with its grand courts, ravishing ladies, bold cavaliers, and mountebanks. In Poland, Hugo's great successor and the first and only Romanticist to win a Nobel Prize in Literature, Henryk Sienkiewicz, set his entire grand "trilogy" in Poland's past era of wars for survival and liberation.

A Sienkiewicz novel that is a great favorite of Objectivists, because recommended decades ago by the NBI bookstore, is *Quo Vadis*, set in Rome at the time of the persecution of the new cult of Christ. Ayn Rand called it one of the single greatest Romantic novels of all time.

Nathaniel Hawthorne set *The Scarlet Letter*, which Rand called the greatest American novel, in Salem, Massachusetts, of a hundred years earlier; and Walter Scott, the best-selling novelist of the Romantic era, set *Rob Roy, Ivanhoe, Waverly*, and all his other works, in the past.

Well, by the second half of the nineteenth century, Romanticism was dying, first and especially in literature, although Hugo reached his peak some decades later and Sienkiewicz after that.

In broadest terms, the counter-Enlightenment philosophy of Immanuel Kant but especially his successors in Germany doomed the Romantic era. Kant published the *Critique of Pure Reason* in 1781, not long after the emergence of the Romantic school; but half a century passed before such ideas gave rise to Naturalism and began to banish Romanticism from the scene. Not surprisingly, Romantic literature was the first to go because its premises are explicit, conceptual, and thus readily attacked; whereas, in music, the last great Romantic composer, Sergei Rachmaninoff, was still writing and performing well into Ayn Rand's adulthood.

Naturalism attacked the Romantic novel with the claim that Naturalism wrote about real, contemporary life—life as we live it, today. By contrast, the great American Romantic novels of Hawthorne, all of James Fennimore Cooper, and much of Herman Melville present values and conflicts that are glorious dramas of human will, with heroes larger than life—but all of it happened long ago and far away.

How did the anti-Enlightenment philosophers lay down the barrage that weakened the defenses of Romanticism and opened it to the assault of the Naturalists? Above all, Romanticism relied upon the Enlightenment profile of man as freely choosing and fighting for his values and facing the consequences of his choices. Kant and his successors undercut this view of individuals as aware of reality by using reason and freely choosing the values that shaped their characters and lives.

"Naturalism," later "social realism" or just "realism" is usually placed between the 1880s and the 1930s. Naturalism suggested that social conditions, heredity, and environment shaped human character. It was mainly a literary movement because, as I said, *explicit* Romanticism was attacked first. Naturalism claimed to depict believable, everyday people and reality.

Naturalist writers and critics were familiar with Charles Darwin's theory of evolution; they asserted that man's heredity determined his character. *Wikipedia* writes, with a simple truth, that "Naturalistic works often include uncouth or sordid subject matter; for example, Émile Zola's works had a frankness about sex along with a pervasive pessimism. Naturalistic works exposed the dark harshness of life, including poverty, racism, violence, prejudice, disease, corruption, prostitution, and filth."

In many novels, today, that list has been whittled down to corruption, violence, and sexual filth.

As many of you know, in characterizing Naturalism, Ayn Rand identified as its archetype the French novelist named above, Emile Zola, who claimed that his innovation in fiction-writing was the creation of characters and plots based on scientific method. It was one of the bigger of the "big lies," but, still, he wasn't writing about knights and ladies and castles.

When Ayn Rand describes "Naturalism" as the opposite and antagonist of "Romanticism," she is referring more broadly to what we call "Realism." Still, the chief criticism she had of that literary school, which she saw as the opposite of hers, was its "determinism"—and the Naturalists were the most philosophically explicit about that premise of their writing.

And so, the Naturalists claimed not only to be writing about individuals who lived and acted in today's world; they could claim to be writing about the true human condition as shown by science. They had abandoned the centrality of the choosing, judging, and valuing individual—the core of Romanticism—for the premise that man's life is determined by genes, social background, or economic class—in a word, fate. Writers, at least those with pretensions to "serious" literature, chose Naturalism; they chose "reality."

As the decades passed, the *metaphysical* reality of man as freely choosing his values, shaping the course of his life, was relegated to 'popular' art, the entertainment offered by detective stories, sea sagas, science fiction, fantasies, cowboy yarns, costume romances, and horror stories.

Okay, this is our pivot point. Take a deep breath.

Romantic Realism: the present, human volition, objective values

Onto this scene, when Romanticism as a literary movement was a historic relic, a 'dead language,' strode a novelist of genius committed to values of the Enlightenment, but still in love with the Romantic fiction she encountered as a girl.

From *We the Living* to *The Fountainhead* to *Atlas Shrugged*, Ayn Rand's novels resuscitated a dying Romantic movement by reconnecting it with its philosophical roots in the Enlightenment. And then by asking: What ideas, choices, and values must shape an individual if he is to triumph—become a living Romantic hero—today, in reality, in our world? In an immediate sense, you see, she undercut Naturalism's only argument: that it dealt with life as it is lived now, not in some idealized past.

But that is a mere footnote when compared with her reconnection of Romanticism with Enlightenment reason and realism. The result is that we have heroes such as Howard Roark, Dagny Taggart, Hank Rearden, Francisco (Domingo Carlos Andres Sebastian) D'Anconia, and John Galt.

Her achievement in *Atlas Shrugged* accounts for the almost explosive spread of Objectivism after the publication of that novel in 1957, its triumph against great odds, and its compelling appeal today. Only Romantic Realism fuses the metaphysical truth and inspiration of Romanticism with the projection of the requirements for the individual's success in our world, today.

Atlas Shrugged not only makes us feel, as Ayn Rand said of Victor Hugo's *Ninety-Three*, "what greatness men are capable of when fighting for their values," but, also, *I can live like that*! Because Victor Hugo published *Ninety-Three* in 1873, 80 years after the French Revolution that is its setting; but Ayn Rand set *Atlas Shrugged* in a kind of permanent and unspecified "near future," where the conflicts are those that face us today, the characters are in our world, and their immediate choices are ones that we seem, unfortunately, more and more likely to face.

In *Atlas*, no consideration takes precedence over the fact that a character's life is determined by his own choices, by the values he elects to pursue. No significant event in the unfolding plot is coincidental. The choices of the characters as they pursue their goals drive the conflict because for Ayn Rand the crucial element of the novel is the logic of the plot. The premise of man choosing, shaping his destiny, is the one she shares with historical Romanticism.

What sets apart her "Realism" is the depth of integration of the plot. Philosophical premises shape characters who act on values and reach the resolution of conflicts in a way that we could outline with syllogisms. Ayn Rand's genius is to dramatize this logic—but always to reveal and explain it, too—as she keeps the plot hurtling toward its climax. The subplot of the mystery that ends with Dagny's crashing through the electronic mirage to discover the secret of the valley begins when she hears the young brakeman whistling bars from a Halley concerto she never has heard—and demanding to understand the seeming contradiction. From there to crashing in the valley, where she hears the real Halley playing the same concerto, the logic of demanding to clarify contradictions never lets up.

In *Atlas*, the probing of the motivations of characters is profound right down to exploration of philosophical fundamentals. When Rearden finds the fatally wounded "Wet Nurse," and is carrying him in his arms, we have *pages* of insight into Rearden's thoughts and feelings that amount to a Hugo-like essay on the tragic betrayal of the young by modern education. The scene is as intimate as a love story because it is one—love between a father and a son—but it carries a weight of philosophical meditation that never would interrupt a decent popular thriller. And, certainly, never interrupted *Ivanhoe*, for example, because motivations were dealt with in terms of categories such as honor or bravery. Romantic Realism means digging into what truly motivates a character who acts on certain moral premises.

In Romantic Realism, the mining of cause and effect drills down through chance, and then human interaction, and then human motivation, and then philosophical premises until we understand how the chief philosophical premises of our age led to the Taggart Tunnel disaster. Romantic Realism means understanding how philosophy and human values manifest themselves in the world in a way that ultimately is completely intelligible.

A pivotal scene in *Ivanhoe* is a joust between two knights in armor; a pivotal scene in *Atlas Shrugged* is Rearden's refusal to sign over his invention to an encroaching dictatorship. Both are riveting and inspiring conflicts.

A pivotal scene in *The Scarlet Letter* is Hester Prynne's acceptance of the scarlet A on her breast because she will not betray the man who got her with child; a pivotal conflict in *Atlas Shrugged* is the refusal of Dagny and Rearden to be blackmailed by the malodorous government bullies who threaten to reveal their love relationship.

But wait! Wait! Does it matter? Does Hester's keeping faith with her lover, although set a century before Hawthorne's time, fail to inspire us with its broader theme—that when we choose our highest values, like a lover, our commitment defies the demands of convention? Isn't it as good as the portrayal of Dagny defying blackmail based on her affair with Rearden?

One answer is that, no, it does not matter. Ayn Rand could idolize the novels of Victor Hugo, including one set in the "Romantic" England of the seventeenth century. And so, too, can you and I. The emotional involvement with *any* characters fighting for their deepest values has the power to inspire us because we can generalize and conceptualize.

Another good answer is that historical Romanticism dunned readers, again and again, with the message that human greatness, the glory of the battle for values, was to be found in some lost past. We might love the characters and relish their battles for their values, but the real glory lay in a bygone era. And so, we have "Miniver Cheevy," who...

Loved the days of old
When swords were bright
And steeds were prancing;
The vision of a warrior bold
Would set him dancing.
"Miniver sighed for what was not,
And dreamed, and rested from his labors;
He dreamed of Thebes and Camelot,
And Priam's neighbors.
"Miniver mourned the ripe renown
That made so many a name so fragrant;
He mourned Romance, now on the town,
And Art, a vagrant.

The romanticism of the past, valid in its fundamentals, does not answer, for the general reader, the question: What values and actions should I choose today to realize the vision of the ideal man? What would a hero today look like? So much of historical Romanticism served the purposes of what we call, today, "escapism." Our own lives are dull, routine, boring; but, vicariously, we can live the life of heroic struggle for values in another era, another place.

"Romantic Realism" means writing about the heroic individual in our time. But surely it meant *more* than that to Ayn Rand? After all, she created a more complicated taxonomy of Romanticism by referring to the huge and popular category of fiction she labeled "popular Romanticism." Detective fiction, spy thrillers, science fiction, and other "genre" fiction she credited with being the only survivors of the Romantic literary movement. She loved such works, perhaps even more as the only new Romantic fiction available to her; she defended and celebrated Mickey Spillane and Ian Fleming, among others. She described popular Romanticism, as I recall, as the kindergarten arithmetic of Romanticism, even as she praised the brilliance of its plots and its unforgettable heroes.

When Romantic fiction becomes Romantic Realism

But these stories, although set in our world, or the future—as is *Atlas Shrugged,* of course—do not merit the designation "Romantic Realism." Ayn Rand points out that their plots, although brilliant, are simplified battles of good against evil; *Atlas Shrugged* is such a battle, too, but the good and evil in popular Romanticism is in terms of crime versus law enforcement, battlers against malign foreign agents or powers. The heroes and villains are in specific and limited roles. There are variations, but this is the pattern. Characterization, character psychology, are simplified—although in that limited context can be brilliant.

The other distinction between popular and literary that Ayn Rand frequently made was based on style. Writers of popular Romanticism often have an effective, powerful style—and Ayn Rand favorably compared the best to that of supposedly great modern literary stylists. But I think if you grasp what Ayn Rand's style is achieving in terms of the subtlety of emotion, emotional impact, revelations of character, evocation of underlying or background feeling, you will understand literary versus popular fiction.

Those issues are familiar to many of us. But I want to raise another question about Romantic Realism. If a spy story or crime thriller or battlefield thriller is written, let us say, with literary merit, and the characters are psychologically subtle and revelatory—say, of the psychology of fighting for justice, or the psychology of the criminal—do we have an example of Romantic Realism? A very fine novel, certainly, and let's say a fine Romantic novel, but Romantic Realism?

Notice that *The Fountainhead* and *Atlas Shrugged*, Ayn Rand's "classic" novels, are about the *whole lives* of her characters. From at least young adulthood, the novels take us through the career, friendships, love affairs, the great central and essentially lifelong conflict of a character, and its resolution for both the heroes and the villains or losers.

By contrast, a James Bond novel takes us through one great adventure, with one beautiful love affair; a Mickey Spillane novel takes us through one encounter with crime. Most, although not all, popular Romanticism is about an *exploit*.

Let me ask this question: If Romantic Realism bids to let the reader experience how exciting and inspiring is life when lived by values appropriate to man's life, then is the "whole life" nature of *The Fountainhead* and *Atlas Shrugged* accidental, or is it essential?

I am not at all sure of the answer. Many questions arise. If a brilliantly styled novel about a professional spy deals with that spy's whole life, not only an episode, but childhood or at least early development, education, and the formation of ideas and values, the conflict running through an entire career, marriage and its ups and downs, and resolution, then, I think, we have possibly a Romantic Realist novel.

But we don't have a good spy thriller. Because when I pick up one of my all-time favorite novels, *From Russia with Love*, I don't bloody *want* to know little James's travails in the fifth grade, his soul-searching about becoming a secret agent, the revelatory contrasts with his brother's meekness in action, from whence arises his passion for his wife. I want to *get on* with it. Drop me into the middle of the action, tell me enough to orient me, then step on the accelerator and don't stop to tell me about James's brother's wife and how he doesn't deserve her.

Even *Atlas* does not achieve the pace and sustained excitement of *From Russia with Love*—or, for matter, of Spillane's *The Girl Hunters*. But we don't care because so much else is going on in *Atlas*. It is excitement on an entirely different plane and scale.

Is there anything in what I have argued, today, to support the conclusion that "Romantic Realism," as Ayn Rand defined and practiced it, has been demonstrated to be the "right" form of the novel? That it eliminates the shortcomings of earlier types of the novel, including traditional Romanticism; that it is the one form of the novel arising wholly from the role of art in meeting those profound needs of man's consciousness that Ayn Rand discusses in the *Manifesto?* For those in the know, is it the only way to go? This is a question, not the lead-up to an answer.

I do think that in the *Manifesto* Ayn Rand intended to make the case that the Romantic Realistic novel is the pinnacle of achievement of the novel. It most fully satisfies man's potential for experiencing all that literature offers. And don't or didn't many of us feel exactly that way about *Atlas Shrugged* compared with any other novel we had read? But that is a comparison, or rating, not a denial of the value and greatness of dozens of other categories of the novel. I am not even sure I have *spiritual room* for lots more novels as total in every way as *Atlas Shrugged*. Or even one more. Do you?

A new Romantic Revolution?

To begin to wind things up, here, I will remind you that in *The Romantic Manifesto* Ayn Rand comments that there is no Romantic Movement; she hopes the book may help to foster one. The book was published almost half a century ago. How time flies.

By the strict standards I have set forth, here, I am aware of no novel of Romantic Realism written since Ayn Rand. Not a few admirers of Ayn Rand's fiction, myself included, have written novels, but their work—some of it most enjoyable—falls into the category of popular Romanticism. That does not mean that all is crime or secret agent fare. Vinay Kolhatkar, in *The Frankenstein Candidate*, published in 2012, writes about a political election with a depth of idea and character and integration of a thrilling plot with his theme. *Pendulum of Justice* by the Dale and Kaila Halling team, published in 2013, pulls off an extraordinary story about a brilliant medical scientist who develops a cardiac surgery that could save millions of lives but is stolen by a corrupt Washington bureaucracy. In both novels are intimations of true literary Romantic Realism and the authors are early in their careers.

My knowledge of Objectivist and other aspiring Romantic novelists is limited (although I am familiar with many of the novels in the sense of knowing the basic story and approach). But if no great work of Romantic Realism has appeared for well over half a century since *Atlas Shrugged* and *The Romantic Manifesto,* then we are seeing nothing like the explosive emergence of Romanticism in the late Eighteenth Century. Half a century later, that movement had "done its thing" throughout Europe and in America, though its momentum took several more decades to decline.

But, as I pointed out in the previous chapter, the Romantic Revolution arose directly out of the Enlightenment, which in a philosophical sense peaked by 1700. For example, John Locke died in 1704. In the next century, this philosophy yielded three great revolutions: the political revolution for freedom, the Industrial

Revolution, and the Romantic Revolution. In other words, by the late 1770s, an entire European and American culture had been influenced by the predominance of Enlightenment ideas.

Our culture, today, has no such philosophical base. Ayn Rand was the sole giant in the twentieth century fighting to revive the Enlightenment and its three great revolutions. If a new Romantic Movement must depend upon a culture's underlying Enlightenment philosophy, then what surprise is it that no Romantic movement has emerged? Only, essentially, writers influenced by Ayn Rand's philosophy and novels. And that is far too small a base for anything remotely like a new literary movement. The tiny—minuscule, really— number of true literary geniuses who initiate, define, and fuel such a movement must be drawn from a huge population base. You do not get John Keats, William Blake, Walter Scott, George Byron, and Nathaniel Hawthorne—to name just a few early Romantic leaders writing in English—by recruiting at one college. Not even that miracle on the banks of the Cam, which, in any case, was recruiting the best from all over Britain and beyond.

Nor do we have the simultaneous explosive emergence of genius in painting, music, and drama that characterized the Romantic Revolution.

We may no more expect a Romantic Revolution in our time than we expect a new Industrial Revolution or a new American (political) Revolution. To borrow one of the most original and powerful titles Ayn Rand ever gave to an essay—because it spoke to the gathering illusions of an entire generation of Objectivists in the 1960's—"It's Earlier Than You Think."

Henryk Sienkiewicz and the Climax of Romanticism

Once, Ayn Rand's essays came out monthly, and, as often as not, mentioned or enthusiastically recommended some writer or specific book, which her readers immediately tracked down. Mickey Spillane, Donald Hamilton, Ira Levin, Ian Fleming, and others were added to the Objectivist canon as required reading. Sometimes the only lead was the appearance of a new book for sale by the Nathaniel Branden Institute bookstore. I once ordered almost two dozen books to be shipped to me at Brown University, where I was a sophomore.

Things were slightly different in the case of the Polish Romantic novelist, Henryk Sienkiewicz (1846-1916). In her essay, "Bootleg Romanticism," now available in *The Romantic Manifesto*, Ayn Rand promoted Sienkiewicz to the Pantheon:

> The (implicit) standards of Romanticism are so demanding that in spite of the abundance of Romantic writers at the time of its dominance, this school has produced very few pure, consistent Romanticists of the top rank. Among novelists, the greatest are Victor Hugo and Dostoevsky, and, as single novels (whose authors were not always consistent in the rest of their works), I would name Henryk Sienkiewicz's *Quo Vadis* and Nathaniel Hawthorne's *The Scarlet Letter*.

That is called "making the short list." I do wonder, and never will know, how Sienkiewicz was "not always consistent" in the rest of his novels.

Strangely, neither in that essay nor anywhere else, as far as I know, did Ayn Rand ever mention Sienkiewicz, again. And yet, there is evidence that Sienkiewicz was the true climax of the Romantic era in fiction. He was tightly bound to that movement and, partly because of timing, he was the only novelist of the Romantic Movement to be awarded the Nobel Prize in Literature (in 1905).

(Victor Hugo had died in 1885 before the first Nobel Prize in Literature was awarded in 1901. The prize went to Sully Prudhomme, a Victorian poet virtually unknown today, spurring protests from backers of Leo Tolstoy for the prize.)

I have wondered if Ayn Read could have read what many consider the greatest novel sequence in the Romantic Movement: "The Trilogy" by Sienkiewicz? I may be reminded otherwise, but I don't recall that Ayn Rand recommended any literature that she would have had to read in translation. She read French and, as it happened, greatly favored the French Romanticists over the British. She also read Russian, naturally, and English. I have no reason to suppose she read Polish. My father was brought up speaking Polish and used to say he could sort of understand some Russian, but I doubt that applies to a literary work approaching 2,900 pages in length as does the Trilogy.   She was aware, as indicated in the quote above, of Sienkiewicz's best-known novel outside Poland, *Quo Vadis?* (1886), which had a successful Hollywood movie version. But I raise the question about the Trilogy, Sienkiewicz's epic of the astounding battles against invasion that Poland fought starting about 1648 and continuing through that century. because it never had anything like a complete and readable English translation until after Ayn Rand's death. In the introduction to that 1991 translation, supported by contributions from American Polish groups, the American novelist, James Michener, paid a personal tribute to Sienkiewicz, beginning by telling American readers how to pronounce his name (Sin-KAY-vitch). Michener had loved *Quo Vadis?* as a boy but explained that until 1991 there was no practical way to enjoy the Trilogy. Ayn Rand, of course, had died nine years earlier.

"To keep alive the hope for the nation"

Sienkiewicz completed the work in 1887 and, believe it or not, the whole epic was serialized in Polish newspapers as he wrote it. He published it during a period when the Polish nation had been ripped asunder, partitioned by the German, Austrian, and Russian empires. Desperate Polish uprisings, the Tsarist-empire littered Polish forests with the dead and dotted the countryside with gibbets. The Trilogy, Sienkiewicz said, was written to "uplift the hearts" of his countrymen and keep alive hope and desire for the nation. It has done this for more than a century through trials that Sienkiewicz scarcely could have imagined. In a very brief speech on accepting the Nobel Prize, he said: "If this honor is precious to all, it is infinitely more so to Poland. It has been said that Poland is dead, exhausted, enslaved, but here is the proof of her life and triumph."

During the Cold War that set in after WWII, when Poland was a captive nation of the Soviet empire, the communists, with a sure intuition, pulled down statues of Sienkiewicz. With the liberation of Poland from

Soviet domination, in 1989, cities and towns across Poland joyously re-erected the statues.

With Fire and Sword, *The Deluge*, and *Fire in The Steppe* all describe the wars and internal struggles of Poland, then part of the "Lithuanian-Polish Commonwealth," to repel invasion. The insurmountable problems, of course, were not military; the problems were factions struggling to wrest advantage from government, the inability to extend genuine freedom to all classes, and a loss of reverence for the values that motivated the country in earlier times. For example, unlike its monarchist neighbors, where the divine right of kings determined succession, in Poland the king was elected. There were extensive (for that time) guarantees of freedom, property, religious toleration though not extended equally to all groups.

The indomitable Polish knights for decades repelled the attempts by Islam to invade Europe; with each failed attack, Polish women were borne back to Turkish harems and Polish men to the galleys. In 1683, to the horror of Europe, the Muslim Ottoman Empire and its vassal and tributary states laid siege to Vienna. The great Polish general, later king, John III Sobieski, resisting all panic and pressure, organized a European Catholic army that not only lifted the siege of Vienna but relentlessly pursued the Ottomans for a defeat that lasted for centuries (until today's army of Islamic refugees invading European welfare states). The story is told in the final novel of the Trilogy, *Fire in The Steppe*.

The great universal themes of the Trilogy are that no nation survives loss of its founding ideas and values, and that the salvation of a nation ultimately lies in the mind of each citizen.

Notable glories of the books are the portrayal of courage, comradeship, and valor in war; achingly intense and beautiful romance; depth of analysis of the moral corruption that brings a great country to enslavement; and the blazingly colorful, complex characters and their moral grandeur. That moral greatness, for Sienkiewicz, was in the individual's willingness to "sacrifice" for the nation, although, considering Poland's fate when it finally lost its independence, I would call it not a sacrifice but very self-interested patriotism.

Here are a few notes about the Trilogy. Young Sienkiewicz traveled in America for two years, around 1876, the very apex of American capitalism, and fell lastingly in love with it, writing dispatches that captured the attention of his countrymen. He translated Victor Hugo's last novel, *Ninety-Three*, into Polish. The translation, at last, of the Trilogy into English required eight years of dedicated work by the novelist W.S. Kuniczak, who set aside his own successful career to do so, and that work was carried out with the financial and moral support of dozens of Polish-American organizations, including the Copernicus Society of America.

Ranking "the trilogy" in the Romantic movement

To me, it is tempting to speculate why Ayn Rand never mentioned the Trilogy. It was the climax of the Romantic movement that she revered, by the author who seized the torch from Hugo and carried it forward to receive the Nobel Prize in the twilight of Romanticism in literature.

Was the problem its focus on Poland's great wars? Among her favorites by Hugo was *Ninety-Three*, set in the war that the French Revolutionists fought to suppress rebellion in Brittany. Could the problem be that in some ways the three Sienkiewicz novels are "costume Romanticism," featuring knights and ladies and castles and dashing steeds? So too is *The Man Who Laughs*, which she called "the greatest novel in world literature," and that is set in seventeenth century England in a world of gypsies, kings, queens, and court intrigue.

In the end, the explanation is either mundane (there was no decent translation during her lifetime or for her Poland could not be "Romantic") or it was fundamental. And that takes us back to her characterization of "the top rank" in Romanticists:

"The distinguishing characteristic…is their full commitment to the premise of volition in *both of its fundamental areas*: in regard to consciousness and to existence, in regard to man's character and to his actions in the physical world. Maintaining a perfect integration of these two aspects, unmatched in the brilliant ingenuity of their plot structures, these writers are enormously concerned with man's soul (i.e., his consciousness)."

That is a judgment to be reached only after a thorough literary analysis and appreciation of the Sienkiewicz Trilogy by a critic, preferably Polish speaking, with a solid grasp of the Objectivist esthetics. I have not pretended to anything remotely approaching that level of appreciation of Sienkiewicz. But it is an assessment that well executed might be the first step in literary rediscovery of a giant of the Romantic movement, almost ignored, today, outside of Poland.

He lies buried beneath a century or more of dogmatic Naturalism (Realism), beneath a century of Poland's political extinction, and beneath practical issues of translation from the language of a conquered nation. The ultimate stature assigned to Sienkiewicz will depend on the outcome of that assessment.

But whether he ranks above Hugo, as the apex of Romanticism, or does not, is almost trivial compared with the rediscovery of one of the great Romantic novelists of all time.

May I live to see the day.

War and Peace: "Big Naturalism" vs. "Big Romanticism"

Because "serious" fiction is equated with the literary school of Realism—and it has been for more than a century—readers and critics seeking "the greatest novel ever written" converge on *War and Peace* by Russian novelist Count Leo Tolstoy, published in 1869.

Well, or maybe *Anna Karenina*, also by Tolstoy. A massive survey by *Time* magazine asking more than 120 of the world's most celebrated authors to name the great works of fiction put *Anna Karenina* first among the 10 all-time greats. *War and Peace* was third.

It hardly matters. *War and Peace* is not just a universally celebrated novel; it is a cultural icon and a synonym for profundity in fiction. It has become a time-worn humorous reference to the obligation to slog through the world's great literature. And always good for an article: e.g., "Seven Reasons You Should Give *War and Peace* A Chance" in the *Huffington Post*.

But perhaps the real test is to ask the opposition. The literary school of Romanticism—the historical alternative and contrast to Realism—scarcely exists, today. Its core emphasis on plot, arising from a view of the individual's free will shaping his own destiny by choosing values and fighting for them, still draws huge audiences to so-called "popular" fiction—today viewed in terms of "genres" such as action-adventure, crime-detective, romance, and fantasy-sci-fi. But the only enduringly popular novelist who is a self-identified Romanticist and whose novels such as *Atlas Shrugged* are viewed as serious literature by millions of readers is Ayn Rand. She also is the foremost philosophical critic of Realism (which she often calls "Naturalism") in literature.

She has identified Leo Tolstoy as the quintessential Realist and his novels as the pinnacle of Realism, from which that school of literature has (following its internal logic) deteriorated to reach its state today. In her book on esthetics, *The Romantic Manifesto*, she writes: "Some of the famous Naturalists attempted to maintain Shakespeare's abstract level, i.e., to present their views of human nature in metaphysical terms (for example, Balzac, Tolstoy). But the majority, following the lead of Emile Zola, rejected metaphysics, as they rejected values, and adopted the method of journalism: the recording of observed concretes."

In *Fiction Writing*, she says: "A Naturalistic writer may sometimes have a good description [of observable concretes]. Tolstoy, the archetype of a Naturalist, often has very eloquent ones. But to the extent to which they are good, they are done by the Romantic method—i.e., using carefully selected, well-observed concretes that capture the essentials of a scene."

I am a writer and have spent a good deal of time reading fiction, including "serious" literature, but between my discovery of *Atlas Shrugged* and my getting around to reading *War and Peace*, I let 56 years slip by.

Comparing Atlas Shrugged and War and Peace

Comparison of the two books is unavoidable. The Oxford World Classics edition of *War and Peace* runs to 1,350 pages. *Atlas Shrugged* weighs in at 1,168 pages. In that sense, *Atlas* is a stereotypically "big, philosophical Russian novel" by a Russian-born writer. When you have finished the story in *War and Peace*, meeting 580 characters, some historical, some fictional—and as the charming aristocratic lives, loves, and philosophical quests of the Russian nobility are shattered by the invasion of Russia by Napoleon's gigantic army in 1812—you get another dozen chapters (although Tolstoy kept his chapters short) of "epilogues." There, Tolstoy offers philosophical explanation and argumentation about the meaning of the book's events. Comparison with Galt's speech at the climax of *Atlas Shrugged*, notorious for its length, is unavoidable.

Ayn Rand referred to *Atlas Shrugged* as a "metaphysical novel"—her attempt to explain the meaning of man's existence, to "say it all"—and added that novelists have (at most) one such work in them. As another metaphysical novel, she cited the grand canvas of Victor Hugo in *Les Miserables* (near the top of anyone's list of the 10 great Romantic novels and, at 1,376 pages in the Modern Classic edition, outstripping *War and Peace*.)

History has its own dramas. Tolstoy, the great Russian Realist, traveling through Europe in 1860-61, met Victor Hugo and read and praised the newly published *Les Miserables*. Among the epic fictional scenes in that novel is the Battle of Waterloo, which Tolstoy admired and seems to have used as an inspiration for his legendary characterizations of the Battles of Austerlitz and Bordino. (Bordino has the dubious distinction of including the bloodiest single day in the Napoleonic wars, with some 70,000 casualties. It also is viewed as the beginning of the end of Napoleon's meteoric career.)

Just as the fate of America is the epic setting of *Atlas Shrugged*, the fate of Russia in the "Patriotic War" is the "plot" of *War and Peace*. Of course, for Russian readers, there was and is no suspense about the outcome. In Tolstoy's time, veterans of that war, including his own father, were still alive. I found myself captured by the drama of the war more than by any character except, perhaps, Natasha (whom I discuss below).

By any reckoning, it is an astonishing story—not least of the decrepit, aging, one-eyed veteran, General Kutuzov, made supreme commander in desperation when other generals kept losing battles and Napoleon approached Moscow.

Every political and moral pressure is applied to Kutuzov to stop retreating and fight Napoleon. His greatness is that he does not fight when he can help it—the battle of Bordino is a partial exception—and stolidly endures universal execration when Moscow falls without a great defensive battle. Time, length of the French supply line, and the nature of occupying armies are Kutuzov's allies against Napoleon's supposed genius. After five weeks looting Moscow, which in the end is virtually burned down, and with the Russian winter approaching, Napoleon and his army abruptly make a run for home. It is then that the Russian army, as well as thousands of Russian peasants on their own, begin guerilla warfare. By some estimates, only 15 percent of the French army of 600,000 survived to exit Russia. In the end, Napoleon abandoned them and raced alone back to Paris.

Like Ayn Rand, Tolstoy held his convictions with an emphatic seriousness in his work and life. *War and Peace* came relatively early in his career (contrast Ayn Rand's *Atlas Shrugged*, her final fiction). Although famous in his twenties for his semi-autobiographical trilogy, *Childhood*, *Boyhood*, and *Youth* (1852-1856), and *Sevastopol Sketches* (he gave up compulsive gambling and whoring to fight in the Crimean War, becoming a second lieutenant of artillery), he was only 41 when *War and Peace* was published. With a certain Randian capacity to astonish, Tolstoy later disavowed the value of the book (saying it was not true to life) and denied it even was a novel. He viewed *Anna Karenina* as his first "novel."

Without knowing in detail what led Tolstoy to that judgment of *War and Peace*, I would identify his famous heroine, the young aristocratic beauty, Countess Natasha Rostova, as a Romantic heroine pure and simple. Just 13 years old when the novel begins (but 28 when it ends), she is portrayed with the capacity for romantic love, glamour, and radiant sense of life of a soul nakedly open to pure happiness. Natasha, played by Audrey Hepburn in the 1956 movie, by the way, has the larger-than-life human "size" of a Victor Hugo character. So, for that matter, does Mary Bolkoskaya, a woman of sainted Christian devotion and self-sacrificing acceptance. And Tolstoy's heroes like Prince Andrei strike poses suggestive of a character from Hugo's novels.

Despite its scope, however, with cinematic movement in its hundreds of brief chapters from ballroom to battlefield, from Moscow in flames to a wolf hunt on a great estate, from the quarters of Napoleon to Emperor Alexander's palace, the events of *War and Peace* are relentlessly chronological. By the end, most of the characters we have met have died; others have changed not quite beyond recognition. And really, the fate of no character still alive has been resolved—unless the Patriotic War itself is viewed as a character.

Morality, determinism, and war

Leo Tolstoy's moral seriousness made him larger than life. I would say that the same is true of Ayn Rand, but history now attests to Tolstoy's stature. He became a Christian literalist, taking as his text the Sermon on the Mount; adopted a morality of asceticism as the path to spiritual salvation; became a thoroughgoing pacifist; and preached the ideas of Henry George, the advocate of the "single tax" (a.k.a., economic silver bullet) to remove land from the category of private property. He wrote endless volumes of polemics as his life stretched to 82 years (died 1908), directly influencing figures such as Mahatma Gandhi.

He came to renounce all his inherited property and to reject ownership of the copyrights of his works (not surprisingly, his initially happy marriage ended with the bitterest hostility on record among literary families). As he was nearing death, he snuck out of the house on a winter night, with virtually nothing, and died in a train station—reportedly preaching Christian sacrifice to his fellow passengers.

As Ayn Rand argued that the defining element of human nature is free will, Tolstoy devoted his lengthy philosophical epilogues to *War and Peace* to arguing a strict determinism. Readers and critics have questioned how that explains *anything* about *War and Peace*, where characters like Pierre Bezukhov (a fictional image of Tolstoy) go through life searching for ultimate meaning, experience traumatic moral transformations, and become apostles of the power of love and goodness.

In fact, Tolstoy's impetus in his epilogue is to explain *war*: Why six-hundred thousand Frenchmen and other Europeans heeded Napoleon's "order" or "plan" to invade Russia. Arguing against history told in terms of the choices of heroes, or "great men," Tolstoy both in the novel and epilogues challenges the view that Napoleon "caused" the 1812 war—or by any conceivable logic could have caused it. If there ever is to be a science of history, he concludes, the causal role of human freedom must be reduced to the miniscule.

The action in *War and Peace* purportedly is driven by historical determinism (Tolstoy was enraptured with Arthur Schopenhauer's book, *The World as Will and Representation*). Tolstoy denied with equal vehemence that great historical figures *or* ideas move history. He scoffed at the notion that Jean Jacques Rousseau's *Social Contract*, or any other work of philosophy or ideas, had any role in explaining the French Revolution. The plot/theme of *War and Peace*, as Tolstoy apparently viewed it, is that individuals go through life—including the most momentous events—deluded into believing that their choices, plans, and actions shape their destiny.

The plot/theme of *Atlas Shrugged* is that one man, John Galt, vows to "stop the motor of the world" to end history's racket of sacrificing the men of ability in the name of altruism—and succeeds. Of course, this is a dramatization of the power of ideas to set the course of history—as they set the course of an individual life. The novel's action from first to last is driven by the reasoning mind and choices of several individuals.

And thus, Tolstoy became a founding father of literary Realism. And Ayn Rand became the redeemer of the Romantic movement in our era: its philosophical advocate, but also—a far more crucial and difficult achievement—creator of a novel that for millions of readers became their ultimate experience of the potential of a work of fiction to move the soul.

Why Great Romantic Novels Don't Get Old

It is an understatement to say that all my life I have been a fan of literary Romanticism; the better characterization is "addict." Ayn Rand has explained how Romanticism can endow the child with a sense of the seriousness and excitement of valuing *as such*—the foundation of any later specific code of values (morality). The Tarzan novels of Edgar Rice Burroughs and the Sherlock Holmes stories of Arthur Conan Doyle set me up for a love affair with *Atlas Shrugged*, which I read in 1962 during the summer between high school and college.

That is a broad introduction to my topic, but today I finished reading *The Count of Monte Cristo,* by Alexander Dumas, a novel of 928 pages, and wondered why it had taken me so long to get around to one of the dozen most celebrated novels in the Romantic canon.

I *almost* loved this novel. I locked myself in my bedroom with *Atlas Shrugged* and read it in three days. I was not compelled in that way by *Monte Cristo*, but I returned to it relentlessly over two weeks and became agitated, today, to see how it finally came out. The conclusion is dramatic, although in a somewhat forced fashion, and happy—but, I am sorry to say, not the best part of the book.

Monte Cristo in the Romantic tradition

Ayn Rand, in *The Romantic Manifesto*, said she saw her role as a transmission belt, informing readers, in our time, of the forgotten and unimaginably benevolent sense of life of the late nineteenth century. To her, that sense of life was represented by Romantic literature, most particularly, by the novels of Victor Hugo. French Romantic literature came late in the Romantic movement, which started and flourished first in England and Scotland, and the Romantic novelist whom Ayn Rand revered, above all, Victor Hugo, published his great novels in the 1860s and later—well after what historians designate the "end" of the literary Romantic movement in 1840. (Romanticism in music, for example, lasted much longer.)

The Count of Monte Cristo is French, of course, and, like Hugo's novels, came late even in French Romanticism—1844. It is tempting to say that *Monte Cristo* has been more popular than Victor Hugo's novels, but that is true only in a specific sense. Victor Hugo, over his lifetime as a poet and dramatist—and at the end as a novelist—was incomparably popular, almost worshipped. His fame was not only literary but political. His funeral in May 1885 was considered a historic moment in France.

In the many decades that followed, though, Dumas' *Monte Cristo* claimed popularity that seems to have exceeded the novels of Hugo. Editions of *Monte Cristo*, dozens and dozens of film and TV versions, sequels, plays, and videogames have poured forth. But in the end, perhaps, quality triumphs. L*es Miz*, since its premiere in Paris in 1980, has become the second longest-running musical in theater history (after *The Fantasticks*). Critics at the London opening panned the play; audiences fell in love and stayed in love.

Buried alive: Edmond Dantes

I am not sure the critics would agree, but to me, the theme of *The Count of Monte Cristo* is survival of the human spirit through any ordeal, vengeance against those who have tried to destroy us, and how in battling evil we risk becoming tainted by it. Ayn Rand probably would not have written a novel like this because of her conviction that evil is not important enough to be our chief adversary. In her novels, the dominant conflict is between good characters who clash because of different premises (errors of knowledge); evil characters are able temporarily to cash in on those errors—as do Ellsworth Toohey in *The Fountainhead* and Lillian Rearden in *Atlas Shrugged*.

My whole heart and attention were engaged at the outset of *Monte Cristo*, when Edmund Dantes, a young French sailor out of Marseilles, is promoted for his competence, with still greater prospects to come, and can now propose to the woman he loves. His enemy is envy of success. The man who wants his fiancé and the man who wants his job act together to denounce him as a Bonapartist agent at a time when Napoleon on Elba was anathema to the new French monarchy.

Buried for life in a dungeon in an island hell-hole prison, by a corrupt prosecutor, while his rival marries his finance when she gives Edmond up for dead, Dantes becomes the focus of a prison sequence that for me is the highlight of the novel. His suffering, utter despair, extraordinary secret relation with another prisoner, and his bizarre escape are unforgettable Romanticism.

But … there are many pages still to go after this. This is the story of how Edmond Dantes, made indescribably rich by a secret treasure revealed by his fellow prisoner, consciously and deliberately fashions himself into a master of the world—the Count of Monte Cristo—the triumph of human purpose over all odds. Human will, not fate, shapes our lives. This is the defining characteristic of the Romantic movement.

Master of the "World's City"

Rich, powerful, elegant, and schooled profoundly in secrecy and intrigue, the Count step-by-step moves toward Paris, where the three men who left him buried for life are wealthy barons at the heart of the Paris aristocracy. The Paris of barons and counts, their lives, their families, and their intrigues are the setting for most of *Monte Cristo* and the literary mastery of Dumas brings them, and the era, to life.

The unimaginably subtle intrigues by which the Count of Monte Cristo ensnares and brings down his powerful foes occasionally left me seeking to recall who is who. If you read the novel, keep handy the list of those who tried to help Dantes, and those who cast him into hell, to track the action. It is worth it, believe me!

Because Romanticism is defined by the assertion of human choice, a great pleasure is always the mastery of life by the heroes—and few ever will match the Count of Monte Cristo. Just as each enemy faces his doom, Edmond Dantes reveals himself to them and takes a bow.

Perhaps the inner conflict in the novel is that to destroy three powerful men, drive them to suicide, bankruptcy, and madness, the Count must affect the lives of many innocents. Malefactors have wives and children. Are you God, even if you seem to have his power, to determine their fate? And, of course, there is the woman Dantes loved—so long ago—now wife of his sworn enemy. And there are the people who tried to help, who gave much in the attempt to rescue him from prison.

In the end, Dumas, who refers ultimate morality to God, does not resolve the contradictions, preferring a final ambiguity. The conclusion for which we have waited so long is satisfying, the villains are undone and a pair of young lovers whose harrowing romance we have followed through much of novel are united, virtually magically, by the count. He has found the woman he loved long ago and secured her future. But his own fate is as elusive as his distant sails upon the sunlit sea. He has left us with the "only truth" we can know before divine revelation: "Wait and hope."

That appears, however, to be his advice to others, not himself—the situation of Eddie Willers, not John Galt—for the count has willed and attained his every objective. He seems to set sail for a destination we cannot know because he created himself to bring justice to evil and that is done. Perhaps it is the turn of Edmond Dantes to live—again.

The Great Romantic Novel You Haven't Read

Ayn Rand, in rating the world's greatest fiction by the standards of the Objectivist esthetics set forth in *The Romantic Manifesto*, named as the single greatest author, Victor Hugo. She also named as greatest *novels* Nathaniel Hawthorne's *The Scarlet Letter* and Henryk Sienkiewicz's *Quo Vadis?*

That judgment might rankle Polish readers, who view Sienkiewicz's *Trilogy* as his masterpiece and, if I may put it this way, the *de facto* literary national anthem of their long-embattled, endlessly torn nation. When Ayn Rand named *Quo Vadis?* it had a good English translation, had been made into a Hollywood movie, and long been one of the world's most popular novels. (With exquisite drama and religious passion, it depicts the struggles and agony of the earliest Christians in the time of Rome's monstrous Emperor Nero.)

Only relatively recently did Polish Americans raise funds for a new, adequate English translation of the 2,000-plus-page *Trilogy*. Unlike *Quo Vadis*, however, the trilogy is "parochial," focusing entirely on the epic struggles of the Polish-Lithuanian Commonwealth (the first commonwealth in Europe) against a bloody Cossack uprising, invasion by Sweden, and the attempted surge into Europe of militant Islamic armies. It was the Polish knights, on the border between western and eastern Europe, who for a century repulsed Islamic invasion and, finally, permanently (until today) ended the attack on Europe by militant Islam at the siege of Vienna.

Readers of Ayn Rand, the foremost contemporary advocate for the literary Romantic movement, have been taught to view Victor Hugo as the triumphant climax and last hurrah of that historic literary movement. Its dates usually are given as roughly 1770 to 1850, but four of Hugo's novels (the exception is *The Hunchback of Notre Dame*) come later.

The young Henryk Sienkiewicz (1846-1916) translated Hugo's novel, *Ninety-Three*, into Polish and seized the torch of literary Romanticism from Hugo, who died in 1885. It was Sienkiewicz who became the first and only Romanticist to win (1905) the Nobel Prize for his "outstanding merits as an epic writer."

As Poland was torn apart (by the Austrian, German, and Russian empires), then reunited, then invaded (by the Nazis), then invaded again (by the Red Army), and then subjugated (as a Soviet communist satellite or "captive nation"), the works of Sienkiewicz were there to "uplift the hearts" of his countrymen at a time they were exhausted and enslaved. Here, he said, is proof of Poland's life and triumph.

I am an ardent fan of Sienkiewicz (and of Polish ancestry on my father's side), but this summer, for the first time, I read his novel *The Knights of the Cross*, which was serialized in Poland as it was written and then published in 1900. With Poland under domination and censorship of the Russian empire, at that time, Sienkiewicz chose to set his novel in the Middle Ages, when Poland struggled against another tyranny. (Later, *The Knights of the Cross* was the first novel published, in a new edition, after World War II, as the Nazi occupation yielded to the Red Army occupation.)

The Teutonic Knights (an alternate English title of the novel), based in Germany, were Christian crusaders who in the Thirteenth Century controlled large parts of the Baltic seacoast. The German (Prussian) religious order proselytized with the sword; their blood-thirsty cruelty to the "pagans" was legendary. Lithuania, at that time, had a Christian ruler but remained pagan throughout its towns and across its vast wilderness. That provided the Teutonic Knights a reason, or pretext, to invade. Their pattern was to slay or enslave all who would not be baptized and to become dominant landholders and rulers.

Poland, although long Christian, had endless clashes with the powerful Teutonic forces until, at last, in 1410, at the Battle of Grunwald, the United Kingdom of Poland and Lithuania decisively defeated the religious order. (It exists in Germany to this day as a religious charitable organization.)

For a Romanticist, however, a historical setting is only a setting. It is not a theme. Nor is a theme the long, bloody struggle of the Polish knights and the Lithuanian peasant masses against the Teutonic Knights. Polish knights and princes took Lithuania's part in the battle against "baptism by living blood." Sienkiewicz made no secret of his scorn and hatred for the Prussian Christian order.

The Knights of the Cross is an epic quest. It pits a young Polish knight, Zbyszko—scarcely more than a boy—against the power of the Teutonic Knights at their most fiendish. Zbyszko's courage and belief in the triumph of the good, of innocence and purity, drives the conflict.

Sienkiewicz unabashedly exalts plot, with more than a dozen fully drawn characters who bring alive the men and women who made Poland of that day intensely aristocratic, given over to concern with salvation, and almost unimaginably rugged. The stakes for which the characters struggle, risk their lives, and (they are convinced) offer their eternal souls are momentous, their all-too-frequent losses heartbreaking. Their values are romantic love, passion, always honor, victory over evil, and heartfelt comradeship.

If you are imagining the age of knighthood, fair ladies, castles, and tournaments, then Sienkiewicz's novel will not let you down. If your concept is of courtly, ceremonious, quaintly ritualistic love and honor, then, yes, that is part of the story—but in the sharpest historical focus and revealing details. What Sienkiewicz adds is a graphic description of the legendary ferocity of combat in the Middle Ages. It is matched by the sadistic inhumanity of the militant Prussian monks/knights in the name of God's will.

There are giants in these pages, almost literally. The Polish knights were unequaled for their sheer size and rude strength. These were days when a great warrior like Prince Jurand would fling himself into battle against a dozen or more opponents, and, protected by armor, level them like a field of wheat.

It is difficult, today, to imagine the vastness and dangers of the wilderness in northern Europe in the Middle Ages. Giant bears, aurochs (wild long-horned cattle), wild boars, and ubiquitous packs of wolves threatened travelers on the roads (such as they were) or in the trackless forests. It all becomes the intensely evoked world in which Zbyszko and his allies must seek the more than humanly lovely Danusia (a "maiden" of only 13 when Zbyszko meets and falls in love with her) when she is kidnapped by the Christian Teutonic "brothers."

Danusia and the other heroine, Jagienka—beautiful, commanding, ready to attack a giant bear with a pitchfork to rescue Zbyszko—have the enchanting capacity of the Romantic heroine for all-consuming passion and devotion to their man. They are the equal in virtue of the Polish knights. To the very end, we do not know whose love will blossom and whose heart will be broken.

Sienkiewicz's novel is not tragic, with happiness and success doomed, but, at times, has the depth of bitterness that goes with great love, striving, and hope. The death of Kira in Rand's *We the Living* and the crushing of Gail Wynand in *The Fountainhead* have the same quality because both characters give everything (in their context) to life.

The acts of moral greatness in *The Knights of the Cross* are Christian, with a stark awareness of the imminence of salvation or damnation. A studied recurrence to such standards as sacrifice, obedience, and the sacredness of oaths causes men and women to act as though watched and judged in each moment. That does not temper the sheer audacity of their deeds. If anything, their capacity for righteousness lends drama to the smallest act as well as the greatest. Daily life is lent a solemnity that gives the lord and the peasant, the king and the slave, stature.

This heightened awareness of the centrality of values keeps the reader aware that at decisive moments of choice, we take our soul in our own hands. This is equally true in any era, of course, but it is the role of Romanticism to make it, for us, a reality we can experience at the most exalted level. In this capacity, the best novels of Henryk Sienkiewicz, and this is among them, do not disappoint.

Who Stole Poetry and Left Us Only Free Verse?

Where I live on Long Island, I have a choice of poetry workshops, one in each town. Our town's workshop meets weekly in the public library. I call it "10 free-verse writers and me." My poems are metrical and usually rhyming.

So, I am the older traditionalist guy in a group of younger poets brought up in the contemporary school of "free verse"? Nope. The average age in the workshop is around 70 and the range is small. And that is true in the other workshops in surrounding towns. There is no "generation" for which "poetry" denotes what I call "the great tradition" of metrical verse in English.

Why discuss "free verse," again? And why now? Don't we have *serious* problems to discuss? And anyway, the epitaph for "poetry" has been written and amply revised many times. Typically, examples of "free verse" from the *New Yorker* and *Poetry* are cited—often incomprehensible, commonly obscurantist, seemingly pretentious—and declared DOA for most readers. The head of a poetry workshop I used to attend explained that her husband would not be coming to our annual public poetry reading. "He says he would rather scrape his teeth on a curbstone."

After citing the off-putting free verse, a typical epitaph for poetry will quote a stanza from the great tradition. The contrast can be telling, certainly, but millions (literally) of poems penned by students over decades that *do* have meter and rhyme would look shabby indeed next to a stanza from Matthew Arnold's "Dover Beach" or William Butler Yeats's "The Second Coming."

Have we lost anything?

Can one make a case for the importance of the "great tradition" of verse that dominated poetry for centuries until the Baby Boomer generation? That cut-off point is commonly chosen because the five-volume poem, *Paterson*, by William Carlos Williams, was published in 1946 and is seen *not* as *first* free verse but as the beginning of the dominance of the free-verse school. *Paterson*, unsurprisingly, was written partly as Williams's response to *Ulysses* by James Joyce. Commentators see him, also, as imitating "The Wasteland" by T.S. Eliot.

So, what of the "importance" of traditional verse? That readers for centuries have delighted in such poetry--viewed it as incomparably enhancing the experience of life and expressing things in the soul otherwise ineffable--might be an argument. That the literary geniuses in each age have dedicated their lives to poetry, even if, like William Shakespeare and Thomas Hardy, they were literary giants in other fields, might be an argument. That scholars at top schools and colleges long viewed poetry as a bedrock of liberal education and indispensable in mastery of the English language might be an argument.

Proponents of free verse, of course, argue that those roles of poetry continue, today, at first enriched—now dominated—by free verse. But there is a fundamental problem with that response. The problem is that free verse is *not* poetry.

What is poetry?

Robert Frost said so, T.S. Eliot said so; but logic, including the nature of definition, also says so. The essential—that is, defining—characteristic of poetry as an art form is *meter*. The poet establishes an underlying pattern of stressed and unstressed syllables, then varies it to achieve poetic effects such as enhanced emphasis or lighter movement. The meter and specifically the *variations* are directions for the speaking voice. And the only *definitively poetic* effects are achieved this way.

This is the first stanza of Shakespeare's famous sonnet 73. The first three lines set the meter (perfect iambic pentameter—five units each of one unstressed and one stressed syllable); then, the poet claims his payoff with a fourth line that piles up stressed syllables (no fewer than seven out of ten) to achieve incomparable emphasis.

•   /   -   /   -   /   - /   - /

    That time of year though mayst in me behold
    When yellow leaves, or none, or few, do hang
    Upon those boughs that shake against the cold,
      /   /   /   -   /   - /   /   /
    Bare ruin'd choirs where late the sweet birds sang.

Why are metrical effects the *only* definitively poetic effects? Because prose shares all other effects achievable by poetry such as denotation and connotation, metaphor, rhythm, assonance and consonance, imagery, sentence structure, and tone. William Faulkner and Thomas Wolfe are modern novelists said to write "poetic prose," which means prose notable for the effects listed above. Another widely heralded example is Vladimir Nabokov, who was primarily a novelist, but also a notable poet and translator of poetry.

We have no problem recognizing these "poetic" novelists without fear of confusing their prose with poetry in the great tradition. But that is decidedly not the case with free verse. I offer this challenge to free verse writers, including those in my workshop: If you did not use line breaks would we know that this was a poem? And not a beautifully written prose sketch or a paragraph from a novel?

There is no effective answer to this challenge except to point to *other* devices introduced into free verse to signal: "not prose." Many writers of free verse, for example, use little or no punctuation. Many eliminate connecting words such as propositions and articles. Most resort to obscure references and oblique descriptions so that the reader's first reaction on finishing the poem typically is "This is beautiful, but I don't really understand what it means." Well, then! It *must* be poetry, right? Because the first quality sought in all *other* writing is intelligibility.

In "real" poetry, line lengths are defined by the number of poetic feet in the verse form the poet chooses. The most common poetic foot by far in English poetry is the iamb (an unstressed syllable, then a stressed one). The poet selects a three-foot line (trimeter), four-foot line (tetrameter), five-foot line (pentameter), or six-foot line (hexameter). For each, there are many thousands of famous models from centuries of English prosody. Each line length has well-known potential and characteristics.

In free verse, line length and line breaks are arbitrary, or, to be more charitable, chosen by each poet for each line of each poem according to "feel"—and justified, when required, by reference to a one-off argument. The destination of this logic long ago became clear, but now is more widespread: "paragraph poetry," which dispenses with the line-break charade.

It is important to mention rhyme. Use of rhyme is limited to poetry (there is no systematic rhyming in prose), but poetry is not limited to rhyme. Shakespeare's plays are written in blank verse (unrhymed iambic pentameter) and there is a long tradition of such verse, including Robert

Frost's longer poems such as "The Hired Man" and "The Witch of Coos." Thus, while rhyme is perhaps the most striking and beloved aspect of poetry, meter is its *defining* and indispensable characteristic.

Where have they Gone and what have they done with poetry?

And so, today, poetry's well-established precincts (school and college literature classes and creative writing classes, magazines that publish poems, and poetry journals) increasingly are inhabited by free verse. In literature classes, at least for now, poetry's great tradition gets some coverage; but, at all ages, in all contexts, the writing of poetry overwhelmingly means free verse. That means, in the context of my thesis, here, that the poetry establishment has given up on poetry.

And so, too, have readers. Today, many people write free verse, often sitting down for an hour or less to produce a poem for the workshop, but *far* fewer people read poetry—or listen to it. In my area, poets, groups of poets, bookstores, and bars (cabarets?) hold poetry readings, but mostly they are attended by other poets. The standard ploy is the "open mic," where poets sign up to read one or two poems. To get to read, they must listen to the other poets. Not infrequently, the total attendance at a reading can be ascertained by counting how many people have signed up to read. Very few names of free verse writers, today, even those on the scene for decades, are as widely known to the reading public as are the last poets in the great tradition (all now deceased): William Butler Yeats, T.S. Eliot, Ezra Pound, Robert Frost, and Dylan Thomas. Poetry today has given up its audience because it has given up poetry.

Although it requires an additional article, a question bound to arise is where have poets inspired by the genuine poetic impulse gone, and what have they done with poetry? Two evident possibilities are that the poets attend "poetry slams" or write, and listen, to "Rap" music (now part of "Hip-Hop").

Slam it, Rap it, Hip it, Hop it

The 2014 National Poetry Slam featured 72 certified teams, culminating in five days of competition. There are permanent venues for slams in many cities. Since the movement began in the mid-1980s, the slam has absorbed new poets and become increasingly "mainstream." In

2017, Tyehimba Jess, a poet who competed at the National Poetry Slam, won the Pulitzer Prize for Poetry. Several slammers have won National Endowment of the Arts Fellowships for Literature; a few now teach on college faculties.

The slam emphasizes personality and performance; slam poetry *is* performed poetry. There is nothing new or dubious about that, of course. Slams have injected the human voice back into poetry and voice, gesture, and drama can compensate for many shortcomings in the work itself. Nevertheless, the slam is a limited window on the world. It began as political protest and remains that, now heavily focused on identity politics. Audiences view slams as political protest events. Susan B.A. Somers-Willett in *The Cultural Politics of Slam Poetry* (University of Michigan Press, 2009) writes that "poems that make an empowered declaration of marginalized identity and individuality are a staple of one's slam repertoire."

Here is a stanza from a poem by Tyehimba Jess:
> when your man comes home from prison,
> when he comes back like the wound
> and you are the stitch,
> when he comes back with pennies in his pocket
> and prayer fresh on his lips,
> you got to wash him down first.

One slam poet and critic, Cristin O'Keefe Aptowicz, offers a partial rundown of poetry slam styles as "…ranting hipsters, freestyle rappers, bohemian drifters, proto-comedians, mystical shamans and gothy punks…" Among those "styles" emphatically is *not* poetry, if poetry is defined by the great tradition of prosody evolved over seven or more centuries by poets writing in English.

Well, has the poetic impulse, then, escaped free verse and found refuge in Rap music? *Something* has found refuge, there! Forbes reports that Rap is now a $10 billion a year industry and "its customer base is the 45 million hip-hop consumers between the ages of 13 and 34, 80% of whom are white."

Rap, unlike slamming, is not even putatively in the tradition of English poetry. It is song, particularly chanting, accompanied by background music. Rap traces its origins, as do the blues and spirituals, to African roots, specifically the West African tradition of oral historians or "praise-singers." Rap undoubtedly is rhythmic and does employ rhyme—in fact, obsessively so, as in the psychotic thought disorder called "clanging," in which the patient connects thoughts chiefly by rhymes and puns. Like rap, but more so, its window on the world is narrow: sex, domestic violence, racism, and a disturbingly repetitious focus on killing police officers. Here's a famous line from rapper 4hunnidGs:

> "Scared to death, scared to look, they shook/
> Cause ain't no such things as halfway crooks…"

I don't think that those longing to experience poetry in the great tradition are going to gravitate to Rap or that Rap even remotely portends a return of poetry's popular appeal. It *does* have popular appeal, but the appeal is not poetry.

The animus against poetry

It is possible to put what has happened to poetry in a wider context to reveal the philosophical "motives," or underlying ideology, of the free-verse movement. The key to the argument is that free verse specifically rejects the *essential* characteristic of poetry. *Vers libre* is "poetry" without meter. No other elements of poetry are rejected, but the element that *is* rejected defines poetry. This has the earmarks of a philosophical agenda.

The analogy with the visual arts has been drawn. What we call modern, or "abstract," or "non-objective" art specifically rejects what had been viewed as the purpose and defining characteristic of art: *representation*. In other words, a drawing, a painting, was of *something*. All other aspects of art—shape, color, pattern, movement, texture—remain.

The thesis is a broad one, but it can be indicated in concert music, too. What is sometimes called "modern" music, to which audiences are treated because government and corporate funders of the arts insist on "recognizing it," lacks melody, harmony, and tonality. At one time, and I venture, still, for most concert goers, those were the very definition of "classical music." Tracing how "modern" music emerged can illuminate poetry, also, for in music there is an explicit assertion that music has no timeless truths and no classical principles. So stop criticizing.

Once upon a time, painting pictures of "something" and

approaching poetry writing in the context of metrical structure were to recognize the nature of an art form, what it was.

In "Nineteen Hundred and Nineteen," William Butler Yeats, the last of the great Romantic poets and the foremost [traditional] poet of the Twentieth Century, looked back on World War I and wrote lines that apply to many things we have let slip away:

> "Many ingenious lovely things are gone
> That seemed sheer miracle to the multitude…"

Cesare Mori: The Romantic Triumph as B-Grade Italian Cinema

At times, I respond to a movie because I love the heroic soul or the defiant beauty of a character, my heart races at the conflict—what is at stake in the drama--and I am captivated by the film's "take" on life—its way of viewing a beautiful woman's face, a pose struck by a man on horseback. And then, I discover that for real film aficionados it is reckoned poor film making. My very first experience like that was with *The Pride and the Passion*, a movie I saw when just a teenager and that I never forgot.

Its setting is the "Peninsula campaign" by the Spanish and English against the conquests of Napoleon, a resistance that began the bitter road to Napoleon's defeat. Spanish guerrilla fighters discover a huge cannon hidden by Napoleon and are determined against all odds to drag it across the mountainous terrain to Avila, which the French have captured—and where they are executing 10 Spaniards, day after day, until Spain surrenders. Only the great cannon can breach the mighty walls of Avila, so that the guerrillas and hundreds of ordinary Spaniards can drive out the French. Well, no more detail, here; I am not writing about this film. It didn't hurt, for my enjoyment, that the love of my life, Sophia Loren, starred with Cary Grant (the English lieutenant sent to help) and Frank Sinatra (the guerrilla leader).

But seeking out the film, in recent years, I discovered that it is routinely dismissed as cheap, poorly made, exploitive cinematography, a weak vehicle for stars, and not worthy of serious attention. But I never tire of watching it.

That brings us up to this weekend, when my wife and I watched a newly released DVD, *Cesare Mori: The Iron Governor*, a two-part mini-series from Italian TV (with Italian subtitles) directed by Gianni Lepre and starring Vincent Perez as Cesare Mori, the "Iron Prefect." In real life, Mori smashed the Sicilian mafia in the late 1920s, with the blessing and support of Benito Mussolini, and Gabriella Pession, the countess of a great Sicilian estate that was the battleground of mafia chieftains and the fascist government.

Uber Romanticism

Soon, as we watched, I became hooked on the heroic black-and-white morality of the fearless Cesare Mori, who, in real life, is credited with defying every murderous threat and plot of the "honorable men" who ruled Sicily by violence; hooked on the countess of irresistible seductive beauty and vulnerability in a society that made women irrelevant; and hooked on the achingly Romantic scenery of Sicily and its people. My wife declared it not her kind of film at all, and I could see why. *Cesare Mori: The Iron Governor* is not only Romantic but unabashedly Romantic. In a sense, you have seen it all, perhaps many times.

Cesare Mori, in real life, was a man of adamant. Backed by Mussolini, whose fascist bully boys Mori had a record of opposing and shoving back, Mori arrested hundreds of Sicilians suspected of harboring or covering for mafia criminals. He besieged towns. He is said to have tortured suspects. He had carte blanche to crush the mafia and he did. He was a man of the Sicilian people who saw that, in their lives, the only power and threat was the mafia—and that he must demonstrate the greater power of the law. He rode on horseback, although automobiles were available, galloping across the Sicilian plains, greatcoat flapping behind, soldiers at his heels, to strike at his targets.

There is towering Romantic passion in this film, but many conflicts are classic: Mori's strong, passionate, adoring wife versus the countess of almost unearthly loveliness and seductiveness; Mori's adopted son, with his wife, Angelina, whose father Mori killed in a duel and who is kidnapped and raised by Mori's most brutal mafia foe. All relationships are at full boil; their long suit is not originality or psychological subtlety.

The animating energy of this unyielding conflict on both sides seems to be Sicily itself, particularly the ancient capital, Palmero, Sicily's premier city. Mori is in love with this land and its people and would lift from it the mafia code of obedient subservience, criminal secrecy, and revenge. And we, too, fall in love with this land and people--the seascapes, villas, and markets—and comprehend that Mori is battling for a way of life crippled decade after decade by crime.

In "real life"…

In real life, and the movie, Mussolini cheers Cesare Mori

in rooting out the mafia; but, in the end, reins in Mori when his investigations implicate figures in the Italian fascist government. He promoted Mori to senator, the highest political reward, but in the senate Mori had little control over law enforcement in Sicily. Cesare Mori died in 1942, a year or so after his cherished wife, largely forgotten in an Italy engulfed in war. Arguably, it was the Allied occupation of Sicily, reaching out for indigenous leaders, that opened the road back to power for the Sicilian mafia.

The film ends before the period, with Mori and Angelina gazing over their new domain, Rome itself, Angelina happy, Mori unable to credit his victory in Sicily, which came at a terrible price and will not endure. No matter. In Romantic art, the goal is not historic accountability, nor depiction of individuals exactly as they were. It is to identify, in men perhaps long dead, that spirit that cannot die because it represents what is best in us. Every major character in *Cesare Mori*, good or evil, is larger than life: more implacably wedded to the culture of murderous, knife-wielding "men of honor," more valorous in pursuit of justice, than real men may have been. That means little. The story unfolding on the screen portrays what mattered most, what values moved those who loved and fought and died in that place, at that time.

"Cesare Mori" falls short of fine cinematography. That is no small flaw. But from the screen, a man meets our gaze, and we know his convictions will make him risk everything he is, everything he has, for a world more real to him than the bitter present. The true wonder of Romantic art is that it matters not at all that he lives and fights his battles in Sicily of the 1920s. His eyes see that which might and ought to be. And that makes all the difference.

What Is A Hero in Literature?

Above all, the hero or heroine has command. Sherlock Holmes, Tarzan, Nancy Drew, Percy Blakeney (*The Scarlet Pimpernel*), Lisbeth Salander (*The Girl with the Dragon Tattoo*), Hannibal Lecter, or James Bond. It does not matter how conventionally good or evil, how lawful or outlaw: Our hero has an enviable command of affairs—and makes it seem almost magical.

The unforgettable hero does not merely prevail—pound the villains, gun down the bad guys, save the day. He or she is great "natural." We cannot imagine the hero, at any time of life, in any situation, different from the great commander that we see. Almost always, the command is mental, because with that many of us can identify ("if I only..."). Tarzan is a partial exception, as is James Bond; still, their characters and their intelligence, in the end, are the core of heroism.

Thus, the hero has intellectual command, but also has a fighting heart. And that fighting heart appears to the reader to be innate and unalterable.

Ultimately, I think, the unforgettable hero to some extent is a romantic (lower case) ideal. This varies greatly (compare Tarzan and Sherlock Holmes, Hannibal Lecter and James Bond, Lisbeth Salander and Nancy Drew). But it seems not to matter: the unforgettable hero is an attractive person; one we would love to know.

- Are there heroes who are not sex objects? Hercules Poirot, perhaps?
- I believe that the unforgettable hero is attractive, in part, by the very fact of his or her command. We would be flattered to be desired by Mike Hammer, James Bond, Lisbeth Salander, Lord Peter Whimsey...
- The unforgettable hero is a fighter, usually a great fighter, often physically--but always in spirit. He or she cannot be defeated, no matter what the odds.
- The hero sees trouble and danger as irresistible challenges, never to be avoided if the challenge is to the hero's values.
- In some sense, we all would like to live the life of the hero: to experience the sense of utter command, the attractiveness, the courage, the excitement, and the triumphs over evil.

The hero, by definition—because of the qualities cited above—is charismatic. He or she attracts allies and is assisted by them. His certainty, attractiveness, fascinating idiosyncrasies, moral conviction, and courage—all cause others to be devoted to him.

Romanticism: The hero is unforgettable detail

In all these ways, heroes are fundamentally similar, sharing an essence, but the details of their lives and personalities are what make them unforgettable. The act of creating a truly unforgettable hero is all about projecting a type, but also an engaging, utterly distinctive individual—one who lives for us from the very first words of introduction.

It does not seem to matter how complex and sophisticated the story that is told. *Atlas Shrugged* is one of the most intellectually challenging books ever written; the Millennium trilogy (Lisbeth Salander) has an infinitely complex and ingeniously integrated plot. Without their substance and weight, and significance of theme and depth of character portrayal, the novels of Ian Fleming and Mickey Spillane nevertheless are ingenious in their plots and their drama. The novels of Michael Crichton have a bit of the intellectual substance of *Atlas Shrugged* and some of the plot complexity of the Millennium trilogy, but their heroes do not emerge from the background—or, if they do, as we read, they quickly fade back when the story ends.

By contrast, we may forget details of the James Bond stories or the Tarzan stories or the Sherlock Holmes stories, but the heroes live on in our minds as real as our best friend.

Probably the Millennium trilogy became a smashing best-seller because its theme is how the individual is screwed by the system, by government—sacrificed to politics. Improbably, the victim, Lisbeth Salander, is a 12-year-old girl who becomes a threat to Sweden's top "national security" secret. It is tempting to try a similar story because I would enjoy making a point about overweening government power. But the goal must be to create an unforgettable hero—or to come as close as possible.

The tough, ruthless, daring heroes of thrillers about government operatives are all the same; there must be tens of thousands or more of them, by now. Ditto with the tough, ruthless, daring cops. They don't do anything different and the details by which they differ from other characters are seldom striking. Every author seeks to project a new and attractive character, but the situations are so similar that no new qualities are demanded. I love the novels of Frederick Forsyth and the early novels of Ken Follett; but not one of their heroes remains in my mind—except possibly the anonymous "jackal." Of course, those authors chose to change the protagonist with each book, consciously declining to create a serial "hero." (The gain is that their stories feel more authentic. After all, we know that James Bond must triumph, and we know that no single agent has a string of such world-beating exploits.)

The *Homeland* TV series goes some way to create genuinely different heroes—one a fanatically dedicated government agent with a seriously disturbed personality, one an unheroic ex-POW turned Muslim and potentially a traitor. But the writers are taking rather desperate measures to distinguish their protagonists.

Lisbeth Salander unquestionably is the chief protagonist of the Millennium trilogy, and rightly is the focus of the titles of the books in English translation; the story is her story and the conflict her conflict. But it is another character, Michael Blomqvist, who keeps the plot moving day by day and he is a lead protagonist in his own right, with his crises, his love affairs, his heart aches. It might be more accurate to say that the two are equal and complementary protagonists: one wildly careening through the story, one moving steadily and relentlessly, step by step, in a way that drives the plot toward its climax. I'm not sure if Blomqvist is "unforgettable"--I don't think so. (Although, in his way, he pulls off as many "miracles" of detection as does Salander, perhaps more.) But Lisbeth Salander will live on in fiction for a long, long time. Relatively to her circumstances, her "command" is just short of wizardry.

In American fiction of the Romantic era, some unforgettable protagonists are not strictly speaking heroes, not moral exemplars fighting for the great values against huge odds. But Natty Bumpo (Cooper), Hester Prynne (Hawthorne), and Ahab (Melville) all are unforgettable, it would seem to me.

The unforgettable hero is an original. The particulars, the details of the hero's personality, fascinate us. The hero stands out and we know would stand out anywhere.

.

Incurable *Atlas* Fever

I have had many decades to ponder why, in just three days, *Atlas Shrugged* seized my mind and for half a century has not lost its hold on me. I know that among Objectivists my experience is not unusual; for most, reading Ayn Rand's novels, but especially *The Fountainhead* or *Atlas Shrugged*, resulted in an instant transformation in their views of the world—the nature of existence, man, morality, and politics--that proved not a passing thing, not enthusiasm or fad, but a revelation that *these ideas* satisfied the demands of understanding at the deepest level and the emotional demands of "sense of life." We had not known, I think, that these demands, or longings, were the best within us.

One evening, my sister, Lucile, a freshman at Pembroke College (later absorbed when Brown University became co-ed), was returning from the library to her dormitory when she ran into a swarming crowd of shouting, gesticulating students. "What's happening?" she asked. "Oh, it's Ayn Rand. She just spoke. We're going with her to the coffee shop."

Ayn Rand had published *Atlas Shrugged* four years earlier, in 1957, and to promote the book was speaking at a few elite universities such as Brown, Yale, and Princeton. There were only half-a-dozen such engagements, but they were occasions for presentations of unrepeatable originality and brilliance. In the case of Brown, in 1961, her talk was "Conservatism: An Obituary," republished later as a simple pamphlet, where I first read it, and decades later in *Capitalism: The Unknown Ideal*.

Now, enters imponderable chance. My sister, Lucile, busy I am sure with challenges of her freshman year, completely unfamiliar with the name "Ayn Rand," and simply encountering a crowd of boisterous students, recalled the name the next day and went to the university bookstore, purchased *Atlas Shrugged*, and read it.

And you don't believe in miracles? Really?

Coming home that summer, she was afire with the ideas of *Atlas*. The brilliant, precocious intellect in the family was my brother, Roger, then a freshman in high school. I did not witness this, but obviously, she passed along *Atlas Shrugged,* and in a few days all I heard in the living room, at the dinner table, were discussions of atheism, selfishness, and reason versus feelings in knowing the world. I was outraged. What in *hell* was *this*?

The Donway children grew up on a farm in rural New England in the years immediately after WWII, years of prosperity and America triumphant militarily and economically. Our prosperity, however, came not from the farm but a business in nearby Worcester, a dress shop that specialized in wedding clothes and became the largest bridal shop in New England. The Donway kids, I think, were aware on some level of the price in dedication, personal stress, stubborn determination to succeed, and consuming attention paid to a business prosper. In other words, we were bourgeois, enjoying the wealth—the new Chevys and Buicks, the December trips to Florida, the summer cottage on Webster Lake—but, again, aware of the effort dad and mom were making. A strain that told even on health.

We also were New England Protestants of the Congregational Church and that is a grave matter. The white spires of churches in every town—not one, but often half a dozen—kept alive an intellectual fire that had consumed so much thought and passion as sect after sect built their communities and colleges (Brown for Baptists), with the likes of the deist, Elihu Palmer, and the Transcendentalist, Henry David Thoreau, challenging them all--but heard and considered. We could go as a family to the Chaffins Congregational Church on sun-bright Sunday mornings, boys squirming in stiff woolen trousers, and return home for our big Sunday dinner at noon, where my mother dissected and criticized in detail what the pastor had said in his sermon that morning.

When I heard Lucile and Roger talking about atheism and selfishness, scorning faith, I was enraged. At some level, I took seriously belief in God, although my commitment turned out to be remarkably loosely attached. For what it is worth, in my senior year in high school I was taught by an exchange teacher from Holland who suggested that I write a paper on *Thus Spake Zarathustra* by Nietzsche—one of Ayn Rand's early and most powerful emotional inspirations, although she later repudiated his theory of morality. It would be interesting to see what I wrote after struggling through the book just months before I encountered *Atlas Shrugged*. But I rate its importance in my reaction to *Atlas Shrugged* as negligible—except, and it is a big "except"—I had become used to having my beliefs challenged (I did harken to the acid anti-Christian message of *Zarathustra*) without throwing the book across the room and roaring: "Get thee behind me, Satan!"

Picking up *Atlas Shrugged*

As I argued (mostly expostulated) with Roger and Lucile about their new ideas, I found their replies maddeningly pointed and telling. Finally, I simply picked up the fat paperback, when they were out of the room, I think, went up to my bedroom under the eaves, threw myself on my bed, and began to read. My memory, ever since, has been that I read *Atlas Shrugged* in three days; I don't recall leaving my room, but, of course, I must have. But I did not mention to anyone what I was doing.

And. at the end, I stormed down the stairs into the living room. Roger and Lucile, locked in conversation as they had been ever since they read *Atlas*, looked up, alarmed, and I proclaimed: "Who is John Galt?"

Of course, it sounds much like a conversion experience. Like being born again. How could one book, and just fiction, at that, read in three days, sweep away all I had learned and accepted up till then? How could this one-book epiphany occur even in a callow young man?

To me, there is only one answer. It is supported by ample evidence from my growing up and more evidence from reading *Atlas Shrugged*. Ayn Rand had discovered, loved, and rejuvenated the great Romantic literary tradition and, in *Atlas Shrugged,* produced her literary masterpiece. When I was growing up in the later 1940s and 1950s, that tradition still lived in popular literature—as it does today. The great gift that my father bequeathed to me was his love for the Tarzan books of Edgar Rice Burroughs. As I think back, he must have held them in the highest esteem. I was in second or third grade when, on one of his frequent trips to New York City, on business, he located used Tarzan books at the Strand bookstore and brought them home to me.

No one who knows Tarzan only from the dreadful movies can have any conception of the Romantic hero that Edgar Rice Burroughs created. There is a reason that Tarzan is a cultural icon. Although influenced by the archetype of the noble savage, Rousseau's ideal man, Burroughs created one of the noblest, most exciting, inspiring figures of manhood—and goodness—ever offered to young readers. The heroism, moral conflicts, exalted command over life, and sheer excitement of more than a dozen Tarzan books never may be repeated. They became the inspiration and fount of courage of my boyhood.

From this Romantic inspiration came a sense of morality, an imperative to fight for what is right, and a sense of life as an adventure where all the battles against any odds could be won. And, of course, the beautiful woman worshipped the hero.

Three days reading *Atlas* jolted my whole intellectual outlook. I immediately could argue (and did!) about faith versus reason, altruism versus selfishness, and socialism versus capitalism. This, I recall clearly. And I went off to Brown University, that fall, brashly eager to argue any aspect of Objectivism with anyone. It was quite a freshman year.

But *Atlas* in three days became the ideal of a lifetime because it answered the question posed, up to that time, by my life: If nothing can be as important as being like Tarzan of the Apes, what can I do? Move to Kenya? In the same way, I had read the Sherlock Holmes stories with adulation. Become a detective? And, yes, I had thrilled to that greatest popular saga of my generation, the Walt Disney Davy Crockett series. Were there still Indian wars to fight?

Of course, I had not seriously considered those options (except, I admit, wondering when young how to get to Africa). But nor had I any vision of the heroic in the life around me. I knew of scientists, doctors, and teachers. I admired writers like Hemingway, Frost, and Poe—and felt a certain pull in that direction. But nothing could ignite my imagination like Tarzan. And I was too young to set aside that vision without a sense of renunciation.

The difference: Romantic Realism

And then, in one novel, in three days, I met Francisco d'Anconia, Dagny Taggart, Hank Rearden, and John Galt. Exactly as Ayn Rand had intended. She knew that nothing equaled the potency of Romantic fiction in appealing to the moral sense of the young. A hero is the exemplary embodiment of a moral ideal. A code of morality in all its integrated actualization and appeal rises and walks in its hero portrayed in fiction. And only Romantic art achieves that end.

Atlas Shrugged, in a sense, slid like a key into a lock with the answer to the puzzle of my Romantic longing. All the most passionate moral idealism I had known, which came from books, had created in me an aspiration, but not shown me what that aspiration might mean in my world, my life, today. *Atlas Shrugged* answered the question not only in terms of an integrated set of principles, and a working model and demonstration, but with inspiration for a lifetime.

The power of *Atlas* to do that highlights Ayn Rand's contribution to the Romanticism she discovered and loved as a girl. What she added to the Romantic vision was "realism," a fiction that portrayed its heroes, conflicts, and ideals in our world and for our time. She called it "Romantic Realism."

As a matter of chronology, Ayn Rand did not espouse her views of Romanticism and the Romantic hero until some years after the publication of *Atlas Shrugged*. I did not understand immediately on a conscious level why *Atlas* had filled my horizon. I did know that for me the heroes of Ayn Rand's novels relegated Tarzan, Sherlock Holmes, and Davy Crockett to my past, to the place where childhood heroes live forever.

Who Are the New Romantic Novelists?

"Anyone Who Fights for the Future Lives in It, Today"
--Introduction to the *Romantic Manifesto*

At times, Ayn Rand permitted herself to write of Romanticism with a terrible yearning redeemed only by her fighting spirit. In the introduction to the *Romantic Manifesto* (1969), she wrote:

> As a child, I saw a glimpse of the pre-World War I world, the last afterglow of the most radiant cultural atmosphere in human history…If one has glimpsed that kind of art—and wider: the possibility of that kind of culture—one can be satisfied with nothing less…. It is that knowledge I want to hold up to the sight of men…before the barbarian curtain descends (if it does) and the last memory of man's greatness vanishes in another Dark Ages.

But this was Ayn Rand, so the rest of the *Romantic Manifesto* was dedicated to a brilliant, inspiring presentation of the nature, philosophical roots, craft, and life-giving importance of Romanticism. As she wrote, "There is no Romantic movement today. If there is to be one in the art of the future, this book will have helped it come into being."

An "end in itself"

The Romantic school of literature--its heroes and its projection of a sunlit world, whatever the struggle required to reach it—was Ayn Rand's earliest exposure, as a girl in Russia, to the new universe of philosophy. She chose to be a novelist in a world where long-term ambition seemed a bitter taunt. Against all odds, she devoted her life to the creation in fiction of the ideal man—not the accepted ideal of this time, that place, but the ideal as defined by a radical philosophy of reason and egoism. That she succeeded is testified by millions of readers who say *The Fountainhead* and *Atlas Shrugged* not only delighted and inspired them, but, in many cases, changed their lives more than any other book.

It all began with an emotional fire in one young woman, a fire that could not be extinguished even by the soul-crushing malevolence of communist Russia. Many decades later, she explained in illuminating philosophical depth in *The Romantic Manifesto* that all serious literature expresses the emotional equivalent of philosophical, especially metaphysical, conclusions. Her term for the emotional process by which our minds automatically sum up all our experiences to reach implicit generalizations about human nature, the world, and their meaning for our lives is "sense of life." When art enables us to experience a world that is the homeland of our sense of life, that pleasure, is an end in itself. We feel: "I am glad to have been alive to experience that." Every lover of *Atlas Shrugged* or The *Fountainhead* will know what I mean.

From one perspective, I think, she argued that there is nothing more important. Emotions are the way we experience life, including enjoying it, experiencing happiness, and the emotional foundation is our sense of life. In everything she wrote about art, literature, and sense of life, she shared her love for authors and works of the Romantic movement that began near the end of the Eighteenth Century and continued through the first half of the Nineteenth Century: Victor Hugo, Frederic Schiller, Nathaniel Hawthorne, Henryk Sienkiewicz, Edmond Rostand...

Romanticism yielded to the rise of Naturalism and Realism starting as early as 1850 in Europe and America. By our day, great Romantic novels were rare except for the revival represented by Ayn Rand's own works. But Romanticism could not be extinguished outside of academia and literary circles; it lived on in such popular genres as detective and spy stories and science fiction, which still dominate book sales--if not reviewed in "serious" high-brow literary journals.

Ayn Rand never lost her delight in "turning on" readers to the best among thousands of popular novelists: Mickey Spillane, Ian Fleming, Agatha Christie, Dorothy Sayers, Josephine Tey, the early Ira Levin... Cumulatively, we see, the occasions for her enthusiasm became fewer over the decades she wrote.

When, in *The Romantic Manifesto* (1969), she expressed the hope that this tribute to Romanticism might nurture a new era of Romanticism, she could point to no examples of contemporary Romantic "literature"— only the popular fiction I have mentioned.

A Romantic Revolution

Reading the book almost 50 years ago, I was not aware of any Objectivist publishing fiction, though some were struggling to write.

It took two decades for the first to emerge. Erika Holzer, a long-time associate of Ayn Rand, published *Double Crossing* in 1988 and *Eye for An Eye* in 1993. Both came after Ayn Rand's death. As far as I know, no Objectivist published a novel during Ayn Rand's lifetime. I have wondered if fear of judgment was the reason--although Ayn Rand tended to be very encouraging of young writers.

Today, the situation has begun to change. One informal list assembled and posted on Amazon includes some 30 first novels by professed Objectivists. Nor is that list complete, I am sure. Why did this take so long? I believe that many had to overcome their awe of Ayn Rand's achievements in fiction and her imperiously high standards for judging the fiction of others. The "Open Objectivist" movement of the Atlas Society encouraged the unintimidated exchange of ideas, criticism of Objectivism, contributions to thought about Objectivism, even contributions to the Objectivist philosophy: that is, Ayn Rand's ideas considered as a now-independent historical philosophical system, with its own internal logic and integrity--not "Objectivism' only in the (also valid) sense of Ayn Rand's works.

Another factor has been self-publishing. It always was available, of course, through what was called "vanity presses," but the name suggests the stigma. With self-publishing through Amazon, the cost of publishing a new novel became vanishingly small—as did the chances of reaching a significant readership. Self-publishing removed the requirement to persuade professional editors at publishing houses to accept a novel with themes such as (to name actual examples) a heroic laissez-faire Presidential candidate, a battle against evil environmental activists, or a thriller about the 1960s-1970s New Left resort to violence in politics.

Two new Objectivist Romantic novelists

I will introduce here only two of the promising new novelists with an Objectivist philosophical base. (I have published four novels and several novellas but will leave them for others to discuss.) I have not read even all the first novels by Objectivists; I hope to do so. The two novelists I discuss here I know well and have reviewed their books at length. I am excited by their novels because they are not easily categorized as generic detective or thriller fiction (although, as in *Atlas Shrugged*, there are elements of the thriller)—the category usually embraced by Objectivists (including myself) influenced by Ayn Rand's enthusiasm for popular-level Romanticism.

Vinay Kolhatkar is the author of *A Sharia London* (2016) and a first novel, *The Frankenstein Candidate* (2012). Enthusiastic reviewers comment that the novels "must" become movies, not knowing that Kolhatkar has written screenplays for film and television and thinks in terms of the "cinematic novel." He began and edits an Objectivist-based online publication, *Savvy Street* (www.thesavvystreet.com), an e-zine dedicated to furthering individualism. Kolhatkar gave presentations on modern Romantic film at two recent Atlas Society summits.

The Frankenstein Candidate is a brilliantly plotted and consummately executed story of political ideas and intrigue in an American election--and a vision of what might and ought to be. Yet, Kolhatkar understands that plot and ideas never are enough. His novel is about what William Faulkner called "the human heart in conflict with itself"--the conscience of a beautiful, successful, and ultimately honest and courageous woman who first must find truth in herself before she brings truth to a viciously deceived, collapsing, and desperate America of 2020.

U.S. Senator Olivia Allen's ambition takes her almost to the Democratic Presidential nomination in an election campaign at once appalling, sickening, but at last gloriously inspiring. Almost. Until her own inner journey toward honesty cries: Stop! It is a cry that rings, too, from the novel itself--a cry to America and the American electorate. Readers inevitably will ponder the prophetic meaning of this novel written in 2012 for the election of Donald Trump in 2016.

Want to know what might happen if a truly honest man addressed the American electorate--the unvarnished truth, truth shorn of rhetoric? Want to imagine a "dream candidate" that is not a "dream" in the usual sense--electability--but an ideological dream? Meet billionaire Frank Kenneth Stein, who runs for president as an independent candidate. The man whose truth makes him a monster to America's political elite--with their media cheering section and their Wall Street crony capitalists and environmental lobbyists--must be destroyed because it is either-or.

This kind of writing, and Kolhatkar's kind of thinking, changes minds and ultimately cultures. Works like this, if they can gain traction with readers--against the inevitable stonewalling of the mainstream intellectuals--can take a revolution in ideas to a popular audience. It is a blessing that *The Frankenstein Candidate* is written in a fully professional style, with professional editing and proofing, so that it loses nothing in the competition with the offerings of the Establishment press.

A Sharia London, as far as we can tell, may take place in London today, or London next year, but the reality of the story is unfolding across Europe. Islamic jihadists, like terrorists everywhere, are targeting their moderate co-religionists who are publicly protesting Islam-as-murder, cooperating with police against the terrorists, or simply trying to break free of the religion of their birth.

Marlon Stone, like most of us, affirms religious tolerance. Unlike most of us, he teaches and preaches it as a college lecturer. After all, there are billions of Muslims in dozens of countries who lead peaceful lives among their fellow citizens. But Marlon misreads the jihadists as standing up for Islam against provocation--and the protestors against Islam as stirring up trouble.

This begins to change on the first day of class when a beautiful, independent-minded, outspoken, and notably sexy woman in her early twenties, a Muslim apostate, sweeps into his class. Her ideas about Islam challenge him immediately, but it is her dream in life--to live Sharia-free and help other women oppressed by Islam--that draws Marlon into battle against all-too-real bloody jihadists.

When Marlon falls in love with his heroic student, Jamila Khan, and comes to see that she is unqualifiedly good--and threatened by an evil irredeemably blind to the good--something clicks. Whatever the cesspit of confusion or rage, hurt or hate, in the minds of the killers, the only response can be to protect what he loves by answering force with force.

Kolhatkar narrates in swift, lean, evocative prose that focuses on action; his talent is to make that action speak for itself of the emotions and the values at stake. When his rhetoric goes beyond even this, seeking a peak moment, it often is in describing the physical love between Marlon and Jamila and of Jamila's exuberant sense of life:

"He knew that he was past the point of no return. He took her breasts in his mouth, one at a time, shifting from left to right like a child in a candy shop unable to decide what to spend his penny on."

Or: "She became aware of the imminence of the final stage of ecstatic agony only moments before it exploded. Quickly, she took a deep breath and ducked under the water. Her moan that would have been audible became a single forceful exhalation--the exhalation merged with the rising globules of warm air."

A Sharia London elevates a thriller into literary Romanticism, when, in parallel with Marlon's external journey, the novel unfolds his transformative internal journey. It is a journey that begins in psychological despair--the frozen grip of paralyzing anhedonia--and reaches by the end robust affirmation of life, love, and assertive action. His guru is his student, Jamila: "...it dawned on him that she was the teacher, and it was he who was the student. Always had been ... It was she who taught by doing--a masterclass in the art of living."

D.K. Halling is the literary signature of the husband-wife team of Kaila and Dale Halling, whose second novel, *Trails of Injustice* (2015), followed by two years a remarkable first novel, *Pendulum of Justice* (2013). Yes, it is all about justice, seen through the eyes of Dale Halling, whose profession is patent law, and Kaila Halling, who is a trained professional writer, and both, who are involved in Objectivist organizations and activities. Dale Halling has made two presentations on patent law at the Atlas Summit.

Pendulum of Justice is a thriller, but, to me, the first sign that a novel might be a contribution to a revival of the literature of Romanticism is that it is not a standard, formula mystery or secret agent story. I have grown up loving such books; I scarcely can imagine my world without them, but, in seeking intimations—however faint--of an emerging Romantic Revolution, I would not point to those books. They have existed in abundance in the realm of popular fiction even as Naturalism and Realism have come to dominate utterly the "serious" literary scene.

Pendulum of Justice has a serious, complex theme: the literal life and death decisions we now are forced to leave in the hands of the Washington bureaucracy that controls innovations through the Patent Office. One can say, "life and death," but *Pendulum of Justice* dramatizes this issue as a literally heart-stopping reality--and suggests how the man of justice might respond when someone he loves is the victim.

Hank Rangar is an innovator and entrepreneur in medical technology, but, today, there are gatekeepers of that technology--and their motives, and the basis of their decisions are as affected by power lust, horse-trading, and lobbying as any other decision out of Washington. Believe me, as the hero of *Pendulum of Justice* comes to see what that bureaucracy has done, and why, you will cheer and cheer at how he decides to react.

Trails of Injustice brought back hero Hank Rangar, pointing to the thriller genre since Romantic literary works tend to create characters, a world, and a story artistically complete in one book. (Still, if Ayn Rand had lived to write a sequel to *Atlas Shrugged*, I would not have judged it, prima facie, not Romantic literature!)

A thriller thrills on many levels: plot and action, character charisma, the veracity of detail such as the technology, compelling power of theme, and even (yes, occasionally) the philosophical ideas at stake. *Trails of Injustice*, for me, succeeds on all these levels.

As in Kolhatkar's *A Sharia London*, excitement in *Trails of Injustice* arises, in part from contemporary events that are the novel's context and launching pad—in this case. the federal government's plan, in 2009, so strike at the giant Sinaloa Mexican drug cartel—especially its pipeline of guns, including high-powered rifles, from the United States. The scheme was to allow the guns to be fed into the pipelines, not stopping them when purchased by American "straw buyer" for the cartel but following them into the heart of the Sinaloa operation. The program ultimately made a lot of headlines--not all flattering!

A Romantic novel is never its setting, of course, but this novel's setting brings into play not only agents forced to "cooperate" with criminals, but deep deception and manipulation from Washington. Hank Rangar, lying low in Mexico after his first encounter (in *Pendulum of Justice*) with a Washington bureaucracy gone rogue, is drawn into the dangerously disintegrating affair. The battle that he and his allies must fight in *Trails of Injustice* is guided, again and again, by Hank's command of a bristling armamentarium of computer tools and skills. I can think of no novel that has done this with greater authenticity, intrigue, and panache since *The Girl with the Dragon Tattoo*.

The action soon immigrates into the United States, focusing on Arizona, ground zero of the real Operation Fast and Furious, and in Washington, D.C. The stakes increase and the desperation of the Washington forces becomes murderous when the bureaucrats try to pin blame for the "gun walking" south of the border on a firearms manufacturer who is Rangar's friend.

One of the great Romantic themes is that of the fearless individual in a righteous cause summoning every ounce of brain power and scrap energy to fight the limitless resources of a government that has abandoned law to defend its power at any price. In that sense, *Trails of Injustice*, like

Pendulum of Justice, is a classic.

Trails of Injustice is a battle fought as only free men and women can fight it: with a conviction that drives heroic choices, terrible risks, and even the occasional sense of gay abandon that comes from knowing we can do no less—that whatever happens, now, this is best within us.

Here, then, are two Objectivist authors, one a team, who have loved and understood the fiction of Ayn Rand and taken the risks of believing in a Romantic Revolution that is still a battle cry without an army. Theirs is not only the daunting creative challenge of creating the intricately plotted novel, with character, action, and conflict-driven by clashing values--and events with clear meaning; theirs, too, is the task of reaching readers largely by their own efforts. Self-published authors do not need to please editors and avoid offending editors and potential reviewers; but the trade-off is that their only allies are readers who discover their work and champion it.

Still, the hope of a renaissance in Romanticism has powerful realities in its favor. One is the historical Romantic movement itself, with literary works still among the most revered and enjoyed. A second is the incomparable glory of Ayn Rand's novels that cast in deep shadow, for millions of readers, the best output of Realism and its variants. A third is the Objectivist theory of esthetics, explaining at a depth and with a persuasiveness scarcely suggested by earlier theories the indispensable role of Romantic art in human development, morality, and the human ideal. The last, and perhaps greatest, is the hunger of readers for the experience Romantic literature offers of characters to admire in a life where crucial values are at stake in a world where wild laughter at life's unimaginable surprises—and gifts--is always just around the next corner.

Poetry: the Supreme Art

I'm afraid I have chosen a reckless title. I do have a definite idea, an argument. I don't intend to "cut and run," as we say about our commitments, these days. On the other hand, I hope that I don't have to man the Alamo. I will be content if you end by considering that poetry might have a claim to the epithet "the universal art."

Anyway, how would you rate one art form above another? Let's begin with this definition of art that Ayn Rand offers in *The Romantic Manifesto*: "Art is the selective recreation of reality according to the artist's metaphysical value-judgments." Art gives reality to the world as one sees it: what is important, what counts, what is ideal (or beautiful or fundamentally true). The image of the world exists in one's soul as deep and enduring emotions, emotions that murmur, or shout, or cry "Yes!" when an artist, or a person, seems to reveal that world to you.

The emotion is different for different artists; the point is, in the first instance, not to choose among different such emotions—what Ayn Rand calls "sense of life" emotions--but to create and experience art that succeeds in speaking to those emotions, stirring them, letting you enjoy them—as though you had been transported to the homeland of your soul.

How art forms reach our sense of life emotions

Could art forms be ranked in terms of their resources, at an exalted level, for recreating reality in a way that involves, compels, and ultimately satisfies a sense of life? Of course, every legitimate art form recreates reality, but different forms. Forms that are so different that we grasp the universal power and appeal of the arts just by seeing the scope of innovation and invention humans have brought to discovering ways to move the emotions at the level of sense of life.

Dance apparently appeals to a part of the brain that stores memories of a repertoire of movements, and how you felt when you made those movements: leaping, flinging out your arms, twirling, falling to your knees, or backing away. An intriguing analysis of dance and the brain appeared in *Cerebrum: The Dana Forum on Brain Science*, the journal I used to edit. It is available online.

Music's appeal seems most direct of all, perhaps because it

bypasses both vision and the conceptual level of consciousness that is reached by language. Vision may be the sense most closely related to concept-formation. However that is, music seems to excite the neurons that hold our memories of certain emotions, so they release emotion the way crushed spice releases odor and flavor. Without knowing how sounds or strings of sounds stir specific centers of emotion, composers have learned to correlate specific sound stimuli with the emotions those stimuli typically evoke.

Drawing, painting, and other visual arts can to some extent bypass the conceptual faculty, making their appeal directly through the senses to the brain, without the intervening step of language. The vocabulary of the visual arts is a vocabulary of color, shape, texture, and visual images, which, in the case of representational art, shows us things or combinations of things that we have seen and to which we now attach emotion.

The medium of the dramatic arts mixes the spoken word, music, human actions and facial expressions, and sometimes certain visual props. Drama is our transition into the conceptual arts, the arts that seem less direct in their effect because first we hear or see words, then we have a thought, an image, a memory, and then those evoke emotions. With novels, the medium is the printed word, or at least essentially so.

Defining "poetry"

The medium of the art of poetry is the speaking or singing human voice. Poetry is not at its core an art of the printed word. When it is printed, it gives directions for speaking and hearing words either aloud or in the theater of the mind. If this does not happen, then the defining characteristic of the art of poetry is not being experienced. That contrasts with the novel, where a silent reading conveys most of the power of the art form. I don't know, some of you may have read *Atlas Shrugged* aloud, declaiming the scenes, gesturing, but my experience was solitary and silent, and it had quite an effect.

What I would like to suggest today is that poetry makes its appeal in its own distinctive ways, but also in the ways that almost all the other arts make their appeal. What is distinctive about poetry, its unique and defining characteristic, is meter—the regular arrangement of stressed and unstressed syllables against which the poet works infinite subtle variations in rhythm. The special vocabulary of poetry is the rhythm of the spoken human voice, the alterations in the volume, pitch, and duration of sounds that create differences in stress, which can convey enormous emotion.

Again, poetry uses many other devices of language—indeed, all devices of language of every conceivable sort—and the devices of the other arts—as I will argue presently—but in essence poetry is about meter. I could say "rhythm," here, but prose has rhythm, as does music, and the concept of meter implies rhythm: poetry is all about creating rhythm against the backdrop of meter. I will spend much of my time here talking about meter because the human voice is the medium of poetry and meter is the defining characteristic. A sixteenth-century English poet, Bishop Henry King, wrote these lines after the death of his young wife. He said to his wife that he was coming to her; but it was his meter that told her so:

> But hark, my pulse, like a soft drum, Beats my approach, tells Thee I come; And slow however my marches be, I shall at last sit down by thee.

King wrote poems all his life and published a book of poems, but he is remembered exclusively for the first two lines. It is not unusual for poets, hailed in their lifetimes, to be represented to posterity by one poem. It is even less unusual, though, to be represented by none.

Here is a different meter, this from a poem by Robert Browning, "How They Brought the Good News from Ghent to Aix":

> I sprang to the stirrup, and Joris, and he; I gallop'd, Dirck gallop'd, we gallop'd all three; "Good speed !" cried the watch, as the gate-bolts undrew; "Speed!" echoed the wall to us galloping through; Behind shut the postern, the lights sank to rest, And into the midnight we gallop'd abreast.

We will return to meter, but I want to expand on the idea that poetry commands all the resources of fiction: narrative, dialogue, character, and scene. Why that does not ring true, today, is also part of my presentation, for later.

Poetry as narrative

But now, consider that perhaps the most influential full-length narratives of all time are the "Iliad" and the "Odyssey." Those would have appeared about 3,000 years ago, at a time on the Greek peninsula when, according to historians, it is not even certain that written language was used. If Homer did write down the "Iliad" about 720 B.C., and the "Odyssey" about 680 B.C., then he was giving form to poetry that had only been sung for hundreds of years. Homer defined the epic form itself, sustained for hundreds of years to come. Greek meter, by the way, sets its measure by long and short syllables, two shorts equivalent to one long; there is no use of rhyme. The great Roman epic was Virgil's "Aeneid," written in the first century B.C. in Latin hexameters.

It has been said that today we don't read much Roman imaginative literature. The Romans exercised the most successful imperial rule in history, for 1,000 years or so. Their obsession was public service and the virtues and characteristics that subserved it; Latin is said to have been the best administrative language ever developed.

The Romans admired the Greeks and felt inferior to them when it came to culture and the arts; they sent their children to study in Athens. But they stuck to their destiny, ruling the world, mostly at peace, and did so for a whole millennium. Above all, they wanted to defend and advance the Roman way of life, and the "Aeneid" was their great expression of that. Its hero, like the hero of the "Odyssey," goes to the underworld in his travels. But there, Aeneas meets the shade of his father and is given a lecture to take home on how Rome should be organized and administered.

The *Aeneid* exercised enormous influence on European literature, but still, not as sweeping as the other great Roman epic poem, "The Metamorphosis," by Ovid, written toward the end of the classical age of Roman poetry. Of all the Roman epics, it is least concerned with celebrating the Roman public ideal. Ovid set out to tell great stories, and, since "The Metamorphosis" took all of history as its subject—the gods, the gods and man, both Greek and Roman history—the poem is a storehouse of classical myths, stories, characters, and allusions. This epic has been said to have shaped French, English, and Italian literature, starting in the later Middle Ages. Consider just one of Ovid's hundreds of stories, "Pyramus and Thisbe." Shakespeare retold it in "Romeo and

Juliet," perpetrating on Ovid a "West-Side Story." He plundered Ovid for speeches in "The Tempest" and in "Macbeth." For that matter, T.S. Eliot's greatest poem, "The Waste Land," is full of Ovid. The influence rolls on.

The tradition of the epic shaped the greatest narrative poem of the late Middle Ages and Renaissance, some say the greatest narrative of all time, "The Divine Comedy," written by Dante Alighieri in the first part of the fourteenth century. He was Florentine, of course, and his poetry influenced the imagination and life's work of another Florentine, Michelangelo, who is reported to have had a great deal of "The Divine Comedy" by heart.

If you want to take gigantic, flying leaps over the highest high points in the history of Western literature, you might start with Homer, bound ahead to the Greek tragedies—also written in verse—and then to Virgil, and then Dante, and then to Shakespeare, who, of course, wrote all his plays in blank verse and wrote the greatest sequence of poems of all time, his sonnets. Catch your breath, there; you've been taking some stupendous leaps, and I'm not sure where you jump next. But as you rest, contemplate that all of these highest of the high stepping- stones have been poets.

Well, I have dealt, just in passing, with how poetry was the source of virtually all the resources of the novel and short story and synonymous with the great traditions of drama. And poetry still represents the greatest tradition of storytelling in literature. Now, it is not surprising perhaps that poetry can command all the resources of fiction and drama; they are after all both art forms of language.

Poetry as movement

I would suggest to you, though, that in some ways poetry can and does appeal to the sense of movement as well as—if in different ways than—dance. Movement, most particularly movement of the body, is in the very sinew and fiber of poetry.

> O body swayed to music, O brightening
> glance, How shall we know the dancer from the
> dance.

That's William Butler Yeats, of course, in "Among Schoolchildren." And this from Yeats, too:

> When I play on my fiddle in Dooney, Folk dance
> like a wave of the sea; My cousin is priest in
> Kilvarnet, My brother in Moharabuiee. When
> we come at the end of time, To Peter sitting in
> state, He will smile on the three old spirits, But call
> me first through the gate; For the good are always
> the merry, Save by an evil chance, And the merry
> love the fiddle And the merry love to dance: And
> when the folk there spy me, They will all come up
> to me, With 'Here is the fiddler of Dooney!' And
> dance like a wave of the sea.

That is not one of Yeats's greatest poems; and Yeats is not one of the notables of the poetry of movement; but movement is part of any great poem, and Yeats wrote the greatest of our time. Many of you will know "The Congo," by the nineteenth-century American poet, Vachel Lindsay:

> THEN I SAW THE CONGO, CREEPING THROUGH THE
> BLACK, CUTTING THROUGH THE FOREST WITH A
> GOLDEN TRACK. Then along that riverbank A thousand
> miles **Tattooed cannibals danced in files;** Then I heard
> the boom of the blood-lust song [A rapidly piling climax of
> speed and racket.] And a thigh-bone beating on a tin-pan
> gong. And "BLOOD" screamed the whistles and the fifes
> of the warriors, "BLOOD" screamed the skull-faced, lean
> witch-doctors, "Whirl ye the deadly voodoo rattle, Harry
> the uplands, Steal all the cattle, Rattle-rattle, rattle-
> rattle, Bing. Boomlay, boomlay, boomlay, BOOM..."

I should not leave the impression that poetry's command of movement is best exemplified by these rather obvious examples. All good poetry is poetry of movement, and I mean physical movement—implied physical movement. If you have drafted a poem, you might stand up, loosen your muscles, and read it, letting yourself act out what you are saying, and feeling. If you feel no urge to move, you might have a problem with your poem. The next lines are from Matthew Arnold in "Dover

Beach," where he took his new bride and later wrote about standing with her, at night, on the Dover cliffs. It is sometimes called the first truly modern poem. Not modern, enough, the Lord be praised, to dispense with meter and exquisite movement:

> Listen! You hear the grating roar Of pebbles which the waves draw back, and fling, At their return, up the high strand, Begin, and cease, and then again begin, With tremulous cadence slow, and bring The eternal note of sadness in.

Moving closer to the present, or as close as I get, when it comes to poetry I like, here is the American poet John Crowe Ransom with a poem that swings with movement, of one kind or another, from first to last:

> Twirling your blue skirts, traveling the sward Under the towers of your seminary, Go listen to your teachers old and contrary Without believing a word.
>
> Tie the white fillets then about your hair And think no more of what will come to pass Than bluebirds that go walking on the grass And chattering on the air.
> Practice your beauty, blue girls, before it fail; And I will cry with my loud lips and publish Beauty which all our power shall never establish, It is so frail.
>
> For I could tell you a story which is true; I know a woman with a terrible tongue, Blear eyes fallen from blue, All her perfections tarnished--yet it is not long Since she was lovelier than any of you.

We must move on, but the case for poetry as an art form of movement need not rest. Every poem we consider will be, in its way, a poem of movement.

Poetry as music

Well, music and poetry, alike, are art forms of sound. I would reckon that there may well be more music that is poetry—that is, that employs song, putting poetry to music—than music that does not include song. Opera, of course, is an entire genre of poetry put to music. But this isn't the aspect of the relationship between music and poetry that I want to discuss today. I want to suggest to you that poetry unaccompanied by instrumental music—and that includes song, for the singing voice is a musical instrument—has resources of sound as extensive as those of music and incorporating many, many of the devices of music.

Now, certainly I don't intend to argue for the superfluity of music or any art form. I don't mean to suggest that with poetry, music has nothing to add. Darwin, I think, first used the terms "lumpers" and "splitters," and I think Objectivists are lumpers, sometimes to a fault, but I scarcely would try to lump all arts and their distinctive characteristics into poetry. For one thing, you can enjoy music, by yourself, with your eyes closed. Well, you can do that with poetry, but first you must memorize the poem. With music, you can lie back, close your eyes, dim the lights, and let the sounds invade your consciousness, past your weary conceptual faculty, and tickle your sense of life. Poetry, I think, whatever its qualities, poetry reaches your brain circuits, the ones with the stored ensemble of sense-of-life neurons--in a less direct manner than music. You do have to hear the words. Still, you only just have to hear them; the music of the words has its own profound power. Let's go back to Yeats and a later poem, "A Last Confession."

> What lively lad most pleasured me Of all that with me lay? I answer that I gave my soul And loved in misery, But had great pleasure with a lad That I loved bodily.

> Flinging from his arms I laughed To think his passion such He fancied that I gave a soul Did but our bodies touch, And laughed upon his breast to think Beast gave beast as much.

> I gave what other women gave That stepped out of their clothes But when this soul, its body off, Naked to naked goes, He it has found shall find therein What none other knows,

And give his own and take his own And rule in his own right; And though it loved in misery Close and cling so tight, There's not a bird of day that dare Extinguish that delight.

What I hear is that the music changes after the line "And laughed upon his breast to think." Until then, the tone is carefree, but almost despairingly frivolous, a throwaway. The music then becomes sober, as she realizes the nature of the pleasure, the huge joke on her men and herself: "Beast gave beast as much."

The music then changes again, into a constrained, rather uptight, perhaps resentful statement, with the line: "I gave what other women gave..." Then, I hear another shift in music when she talks about the transition from bodily existence and pleasures to pleasures beyond and apart from the body: real nakedness, the nakedness of the soul, with the line "Naked to naked goes."

Here, the music assumes a tone of the most intense dedication, the vow of the novitiate to her god: "He it has found shall found therein..." It has an almost desperate sincerity: "Close and cling so tight..." and only lightens at the end, as the new pleasure, this time ecstasy, awakens: "There's not a bird of day that dare/Extinguish that delight." The woman who has been the pleasure toy of beasts now gazes upon herself in the embrace of God.

The enchantment of the sound comes in part from the varying rhythm, as we shall see with other poems. But any poem, as it rises in intensity, increases the number of syllables that are stressed.

Scanning, of course, is the identification of the stressed and unstressed syllables in a line and dividing them into the standard measures, or "feet" of English poetry.

FLING ing from his ARMS, I LAUGHED...

I hear three stressed syllables, here, and four unstressed. But "laughed" is one of those long single-syllables words that almost become two syllables. After that, the stresses pile up, as her voice gains intensity, especially the vision of submission to God:

We have the music of the balanced "l" sounds in the line "Flinging from his arms, I laughed..." And we have the same balance of the "r" sounds in the line "And rule in his own right..." We have the emphatic bringing down of the fist in the "d" sounds in "Not a bird of day that dare..." that is echoed by the final word, "delight."

The music of the rhyme scheme here is intense because groups of three rhyming words are used. English is a relatively rhyme-poor language. It is doubtful any poet in English could have written the thousands and thousands of rhyming lines of *The Divine Comedia*, for which Dante had available the thousands of words endings with "ia" and other vowel sounds in Italian. By contrast, the English poet wonders how he can possibly use "life" in a line within a poem not about marriage or stabbing and not slightly archaic in tone, so he can rhyme with "wife," "knife," or "strife." At any rate, Yeats uses rhymes so naturally and beautifully that you may not have realized that he was using triple rhymes. And in the final stanza, the rhymes are three of the most significant terms in the stanza and the poem: "right," "tight," and "delight."

I could mention much, much more about the music of the sounds in this poem. For example, Yeats must have sensed it was very desirable to end the poem with a word that included an "l" sound to echo the many important words in the poem that share that sound: "lady," "lad," lively," "pleasured," "lay," "soul," "loved," "flinging," "laughed," "rule," "close," and "cling"—among others. Note that in the first half of the poem the many, many more "l" sounds are in words that lilt—lively, like the lady. In the second half, the few "l" words are either not especially significant, like "shall" or definitely not lilting—for example, "rule." Only at the end is the lost joy once again regained, this time by the soul, with the lilting word "delight."

Poetry as a visual art

Now, I would not try to take anything away from painting, which, like music, has a direct and immediate effect on the emotions that the art forms of language do not—at least, insofar as they are concerned with concepts, not sound and rhythm, which do have a quite direct effect. But painting and drawing appeal to our dominant sense, vision, and when poetry conjures up images in words, the effect of the words depends upon our having stored the original image in our memory. So give the visual arts their due. Except, of course, that the images they can use are quite severely limited as compared with poetry.

I used "image" to mean any directly experienced quality in our stream of consciousness. In that usage, all the senses contribute to our imagery. We have direct awareness of visual images, but also sound images. You are forming images of my voice; you can hear in your mind the particular qualities of the sound I use for "Yeats." Likewise, you can have an olfactory image or a tactile image. Well, the visual arts do not convey any but visual images. Yes, you can associate images from other senses with what you see in a painting: a cherry almost real and ripe and red enough to taste. But poetry can evoke, deliberately and with considerable definition, images from any of the five senses and from proprioception and interoception—the experience of the position of your limbs, your body in space, and other perceptions from within you. Further, poetry can evoke a mixture of the senses; it can evoke a sequence of sensations; and, above all, it can evoke images that might be termed abstract images.

Don't even think about a painting that might capture this striking and disturbing image from Yeats's "Crazy Jane Talks to the Bishop."

> A woman can be proud and stiff When
> on love intent But Love has pitched his
> mansion In the place of excrement And
> nothing can be sole or whole That has not
> been rent.

This is from Ezra Pound's "Ballad of the Goodly Fere," about Christ and the apostles. Simon speaks it after the crucifixion:

> He cried no cry when they drave the
> nails And the blood gushed hot and free The
> hounds of the crimson sky gave tongue But
> never a cry cried he.

We have the immediate visual image of the blood, but the image is of its movement—spurting—and its temperature—hot. The next image is partly visual, partly acoustic, and partly even abstract: "The hounds of the crimson sky gave tongue..." I see long, dark clouds of red and purple on the horizon behind the hill at Calvary, and they are low and stretched, like running hounds, their tongues lolling, and their howl is not in the sky but the mind of Simon, to whom the whole scene is so unbearable that he knows not whether he or the heavens will howl first. Note the music in the three long "o's" of "hounds," "crimson," and "tongue," which roll and moan like far-off thunder. Then we switch to the high-pitched vowels of "cry cried he"--ending in the "e" that is almost itself a cry. That's a lot for one or two lines of imagery.

How could you capture visually the image that begins "The Love Song of J. Alfred Prufrock":

> When the evening is spread out against the sky Like a patient, etherized upon a table...

Eliot was inviting you upon a tour of a world in which the romanticism of evening skies, and the strolls of lovers through charming cities at dusk, no longer could be taken seriously. A patient in the operating room under ether has cheeks flushed pink like the evening sky. Eliot's sky is at best sedated, but more probably gravely afflicted, life hanging in the balance; the age itself is the patient, Eliot will make the diagnosis. The patient on the gurney and the evening sky, presumably over Boston, are brought together in one image, united by their pink hue, the impending night, and the admitted and accepted lack of romance.

Well, I want to spend a little time specifically on meter, the defining characteristic of poetry, and a little on the state of modern poetry. But "At my back I hear time's winged chariot hurrying near..."

The measure of meter

"Meter" means "measure" and poets writing in English take the measure of the rhythm of their lines by reference to units called feet. English meter, and metrical feet, are units defined both by the number of syllables and the placement of stressed and unstressed syllables. A list of metrical feet may be longer or shorter, but the shortest, reduced to essentials, is as follows:

iamb (unstressed and STRESSED: e LOPE trochee
(STRESSED and unstressed): LOV er spondee
(STRESSED, STRESSED): CUCK OLD anapest
(unstressed, unstressed, STRESSED): to the
WOODS dactyl (STRESSED, unstressed, unstressed): PAS
sion ate pyrrhic (unstressed, unstressed): [TURN ing and
TURN] in the [WID en ing] GYRE

To use single, out-of-context words as examples of the feet is
misleading. The syllables around the word might affect how it is stressed;
and meaning might affect how it is stressed. For example, I might use as
an example "worn out" and call it an iamb: worn OUT.

But that would change if I wrote: "I didn't say I was BORN out of
wedlock. I said I was WORN out with wedlock." It is a skill and an art,
even a high art, to scan poetry. There have been masters such as the poet
Yvor Winters; a classic on the subject was written by Paul Fussell. After
all, do any two syllables have exactly the same stress? Above, I used as an
example of a dactyl the word PAS sion ate. One stressed syllable followed
by two unstressed. But relatively, to my ear, the final syllable is stressed a
bit more than the middle syllable.

How you divide a line into metrical feet can be debated like the
abilities and sex appeal of two actresses. The pyrrhic, two unstressed
syllables, is impossible to use except as a variation because it always
can be divided up between the preceding and following feet. And some
mavens of scanning like to use additional feet, with four syllables. But
these, too, can always be divided into two feet or redistributed.

The far more pressing decision for the poet is to choose a
meter (and more than 90 percent of the time it will be iambic, the
overwhelmingly dominant meter in serious English poetry) and a
line length. If the line length is five feet, then the poet is using iambic
pentameter, the runaway favorite in all English poetry, the line of
Shakespeare's sonnets, the line of all the great poems in blank verse
(unrhymed iambic pentameter), and often said to be the natural beat of
spoken English.

The skillful poet will keep this underlying beat, like a metronome,
and vary it to achieve his effects and create his rhythm. The variations in
effects achievable by varying iambic pentameter have not been exhausted

by millions of lines of English poetry written over more than 500 years. When variations in rhythm are combined with the resources of meaning, tone, mood, rhyme, vowel- and consonant-repetitions (assonance and consonance) and all the other resources of poetry, there is no end in sight.

The poet will establish his meter and keep returning to it throughout the poem. If he lets the variations go on too long, the underlying beat may be lost, and so the variations cease to be variations. If he lets the meter go on too long, he risks a metronome regularity, and rhythm is made by the piano, not the metronome. He will keep tightening and loosening; but, a cardinal feature of poetry is that as the intensity of the statement increases, the stresses will come closer together, building emphasis and tension:

> STAND, STAND at the WIN dow As the TEARS SCALD and START You must LOVE your CROOKED NEIGH bor With your CROOKED HEART.

> LOOK, LOOK in the MIR ror LOOK, in your disTRESS LIFE re MAINS a BLESS ing Al THOUGH YOU CANNOT BLESS.

W. H. Auden's wonderful poem "As I Walked Out One Evening," has an iambic meter, so the underlying beat is unstressed, STRESSED, unstressed, STRESSED, unstressed STRESSED. And for much of the poem that meter is sustained:

> Oh LET not TIME de CEIVE you, You CAN not CON quer TIME.

In fact, for much of the poem, the unstressed syllables predominate; there are many anapests, a frequent variation in iambic lines:

> And a CRACK in the TEA cup O pens, A LANE to the LAND of the DEAD, Where the BEG ars RAF fle the BANK notes, And the GIANT is en CHANT ing to JACK...

I would say the meter is iambic, made less formal and more conversational by the use of the extra unaccented syllables in anapests.

But look again at that climax:

> STAND, STAND at the WIN dow As the TEARS SCALD and START YOU must LOVE your CROOKED NEIGH bor With your CROOKED HEART.
>
> LOOK, LOOK in the MIR ror Oh, LOOK, in YOUR disTRESS LIFE re MAINS a BLESS ing Al THOUGH YOU CANNOT BLESS.

The iambic beat, established earlier in this long poem, is left behind in the clustering of stresses in the poet's climactic exhortation to hold onto compassion, to love, and struggle against renunciation. Virtually all moments of high intensity and drama in poetry are expressed in this build-up of stresses. Yes, I could have scanned differently, marking "you" and "not" in the last line as unstressed. It depends upon how you speak the lines. I read the meaning as "Although YOU cannot bless." In other contexts, "cannot" would receive the stress only on the "can." If you do stress "you," I think that "not" probably should be unstressed. Notice, though, that these decisions change not at all the clear character of the passages, as the poet piles on emphasis, urgently pleading for self-examination in the teeth of despair.

One more example of meter, this from a famous sonnet by Shakespeare. The scanning of the passage has been much debated:

> That time of year though mayst in me behold, When yellow leaves, or none, or few, do hang Upon those boughs which shake against the cold, Bare ruin'd choirs, where late the sweet birds sang.

There is no debate whatsoever about the first three lines. They are perfect iambic pentameter. No other scanning is even plausible. Shakespeare is setting up a powerful underlying beat. For a textbook example of iambic pentameter it is impossible to improve on the second line::When yellow leaves, or none, or few, do hang..." Note this shivery imagery, and how the unfolding of the image gives it poignancy. By adding "or few," the poet in two words has reminded us how as we age we watch our inevitable losses—the last few strands of hair, the few remaining old friends. But onward to the meter and rhythm of this poem:

> That TIME of YEAR though MAYST in ME be
> HOLD, When YEL low LEAVES, or NONE, or FEW, do
> HANG U PON those BOUGHS which SHAKE a GAINST
> the COLD, BARE RUIN'D CHOIRS, where LATE the
> SWEET BIRDS SANG.

Here is a kind of climax, too, although a quieter one. Notice that the first three words of the last line are single-syllables words, but with long vowels. "Ruin'd" has almost the length of two syllables. The "r" sound in each word also stretches out the sound. We have seven stressed syllables out of nine, here—a powerful variation from perfect iambic feet in the first three lines. But notice that in contrast to the low, long, mournful first three words, the last three are quicker and crisper: "sweet birds sang." Unlike the "r" sounds that drew out the first three syllables, the words "sweet" and "sang" end in letters that snip sound short. Arguments have been made that this line should be given a more nearly iambic scan: "Bare RU in'd CHOIRS, where LATE the SWEET birds SANG." Also, the nature of the image has been debated. Is "bare ruin'd choirs supposed to refer back to "boughs," creating a metaphor: are the boughs the ruined choirs of the summer birds? Or are we looking at the tumbled-down walls of a church in the forest, the last autumn leaves falling on the exposed and crumbling choir loft? Well, the tension and uncertainty, both in rhythm and imagery, add to the tension in this line, making it come brilliantly alive.

The art of anti-poetry

Briefly, now, what about poetry today? My presentation, and several others, could have been devoted to the postmodernism dismantling of poetry as an art form. This has exactly paralleled the dismantling of the visual arts and music. As you know, the postmodernists always go for the jugular, for the lifeline of the art, and slash that. In painting, the attack was on representation, in music the attack was on melody. In poetry, the attack has been on meter—the defining essence of the art form. Free verse is the abandonment of meter. Free verse has rhythm, certainly, but so does prose. Yet, what I want to say, now, is not about the postmodernist attack, per se.

The question I posed much earlier was why it seems odd today to say that poetry commands all the narrative power and resources of fiction. It seems odd because the practice of poetry today has, to a fair approximation, been reduced to one minor sub-form of the art. The lyric was a brief, intense expression of emotion in a poem intended to be accompanied by the lyre. It is a beautiful form, the lyric; but I suggest to you that most of what the public knows, and thinks, about the art of poetry is only about the lyric. Today, a poem can be defined as "a unit of writing short enough to fit into the filler space between articles in a magazine." It gets all emotional and imagistic and perhaps reaches some wise point or observation, then ends. It seems selective in its language, but the selectively appears to make the meaning cryptic.

Where are the epics, today—the heroic accounts of the things that have mattered to our civilization? Where are the plays in verse, the great poetic dramas? Where are the satires? Pope, Dryden, and Swift penned some of the most caustic and telling political, cultural, and social criticism of their day--in verse. Do we have no political figures today, no celebrities, appropriate for satire that pricks pretension, catches sheer political frivolity in the act, or punctures the idols of the current theater or arts? In short, where were the major poetic forms and traditions of some 3,000 years that created the most memorable literature in our entire civilization? Where for that matter are the philosophical works in verse like *De Rerum Natura*, "On the Nature of Things," written in the first century B.C. by the Roman Epicurean philosopher and scientist, Lucretius? His goal was to free men from religious superstition and so from the fear of death. Where are even the kind of dramatic monologues written by Robert Browning?

I acknowledge a few exceptions, or partial exceptions, in fairly recent times. But, today, the whole art of poetry, certainly in the public mind, is minor. If poets produce only brief cries from the heart—even on the generous assumption these are not unrhymed, not metrical, and obscure—then poetry will have a small place in our lives. Certainly, poetry will have no public role of any kind. How many of you in the past five years have purchased a book of poetry by a new, contemporary poet? I'm not sure that I can raise my hand.

Today, it has become difficult even to imagine what we are missing in many walks of life: what it would be like to live in a free society, what it would be like to have principled statesmen, what it would be like to have unbounded enterprise, what it would be like to have universities founded on a rational philosophy, what it would be like to have a culture of romantic art. Gazing upon that field of devastation, the collapse of poetry may seem a less than life-threatening blow. But that may be because in this field, least of all, can we envision what we are missing: what it would be like to have a great poet to tell us who we have been, who we are, and who we could be.

Ayn Rand remarked wistfully that for those born in the second half of the twentieth century, it was impossible to imagine the sense of life of European and American culture before World War I--the optimism and benevolence and confidence in civilized standards. I am talking about such a loss in the realm of poetry. In his poem, "Nineteen Hundred and Nineteen," Yeats wrote:

> Many ingenious lovely things are gone That seemed sheer miracle to the multitude.

Today, one of them is the great tradition of poetry—the supreme art.

Tarzan and the Hero Within Us

As I write this, Disney/Pixar Studios is planning to treat movie-goers to *Incredibles 2*. The name might be the only one left that can top "Batman," "Superman," "Spider-Man," "Hulk," "Iron Man," and "X-Man." How do you trump that list? "Ineffable" might be accurate enough, but…um…not right for the audience.

Not one of them holds much interest for me. And that is odd, because, as early as third grade, a superhero bequeathed to me a sense of self that sustained a troubled kid through some hard times, instilled a love of the moral hero latent in all of us, and a Romantic conviction that right must prevail. Now, in my 70's, much is gone, but that remains.

On one of his periodic trips to New York City, my dad dropped into the legendary Strand Bookstore and brought home a worn, spine-busted book of an indeterminate gray-green hue on which you barely could read *Tarzan of the Apes*. Only one copy available. A first edition published in 1914--and looking all of 40 years old.

When dad had read the Tarzan books, they were a new sensation. Edgar Rice Burroughs, a drifter who held 17 jobs before he was 37, picked up his pen because he found pulp magazine fiction so laughable, he knew he could do no worse.

He did better. By the end of the 1940s, he had transformed the genre of superhero fiction, created a character whose name remains synonymous with heroic strength and exotic adventure, and launched a Hollywood empire.

My dad read to me. I sat beside him on the couch and listened. I doubt he ever fathomed the extent of my transportation to the Belgian Congo, the turn of the Nineteenth Century, the "upper terraces" of the jungle giants through which Tarzan hurtled beneath a tropical moon, and the victory cry of the bull ape standing with one foot on the still form of numa, the lion.

Eventually, we went through more than a dozen volumes. By then, however, for most kids, the Tarzan books had been superseded by the comic books and by Johnny Weissmuller, a Romanian five-star Olympic swimming medalist, in talking movies starting in 1940.

Any lover of Tarzan, even a boy of 12, could only cringe at the movies. Tarzan cannot be portrayed in real-life cinema. Your character cannot be naked, speak the language of the "great apes" (as described, not an actual species), battle gorillas and lions with a knife, or plausibly "swing through the trees."

The noble savage

A fictional character does not seize the imagination and stir the longings of millions of readers without striking deeply resonant chords. Burroughs never lets us forget that Tarzan is Rousseau's noble savage. Untouched by civilization, he has none of its multitudinous flaws, sins, weaknesses, and hypocrisies. Those unfamiliar with Tarzan of the books cannot realize the power of this theme. For good measure, he is also the son of the British Lord Greystoke, killed by the apes that then took his infant son.

I wanted nothing more than to be Tarzan. Many things that make real childhood less than the Eden of our later memories call for courage and self-esteem. Are courage and self-esteem "real" when they emanated from an inner self-image as Tarzan? In small towns of the late '40s and early '50s, among mostly farm boys, bullying was endemic. To oppose it, parents risked accusations of "babying," not letting "boys be boys," not "letting the kids work it out."

Against whatever odds when I fought back it was Tarzan fighting back. Moreover, Tarzan was a champion of the victimized and beset— and so, in a way, that is what I became. Although in serious literature, the Romantic tradition of value-clashes of heroes and villains portrayed in terms now denigrated as "black-and-white" (evil and good) ended in the 1850s (later in France with the novels of Victor Hugo), Romanticism never died out in popular fiction.

What it gives to young readers might be termed a "sense of values"—not any specific values or moral code, but the sense that life is about pursuing and fighting for values. Later, that sense of values is populated by a specific moral code whether secular liberal humanism or religious fundamentalism.

Tarzan on my mind

As I write this, I am aware that I largely have failed to project the reality of Tarzan to those unfamiliar with the books. But I can take a final shot at evoking my boyhood world of Tarzan. These are a few stanzas of a poem I wrote to capture the sense I had of being in the world of Tarzan:

> You would appear upon my path,
> As sun will touch a single tree;
> And with your eyes as wild and kind
> As freedom, you would look on me,
>
> And nod, impartial as a beast,
> Or God, and I would go, and soon
> We'd fly as high as dream desire
> Through trees beneath a jungle moon.
>
> And we would never tire, fight
> And never doubt. Our fathers' knives,
> Baptized in fierce Bolgani's blood,
> Would bless the battles of our lives.
>
> We'd summon good Tantor and tease
> Malicious Sheetah's snarling smile.
> We'd stride as nude and beautiful
> As beasts to baffle Satan's guile.
>
> At manhood's noon, our two great hearts
> Would stay the lion's breath above
> The golden woman's blameless breast,
> And slay the lord of Death—for love.

A comment on Edgar Rice Burroughs

Readers may have encountered criticism of Burroughs. He was a man of his time. Writing during World War I, he characterized Germans in the same sweeping, scornful cultural generalizations as did Rudyard Kipling, who wrote a contemporary history of the "Great War."

Most damagingly, Burroughs is accused of racism in portraying black Africans. He did refer to cannibal tribes as "degraded," but Tarzan's allies, the "Waziri," probably modeled on the Maasai tribe, are the equal of Tarzan as "noble savages." In the massive slave trade conducted in

East Africa by Arab slavers and their willing or unwilling black allies, the Maasai were known to resist at all costs attempts by slavers to buy or steal their women and children. That was not true of all tribes.

I am a novelist as well as a poet and have outlived the copyright on the Tarzan books. This year, inspired by research on slavery in Africa early in the Twentieth Century—particularly the horrors of King Leopold in the ill-named Congo Free State and the millions of Africans who died or were sold into slavery on Zanzibar island in the Indian Ocean—I wrote my own Tarzan novel: *Tarzan in the Heart of Darkness*.

In it, I portray young Tarzan in alliance with a courageous Maasai girl in pitched battles with slavers in the Belgian Congo rubber plantations and copper mines and slavery auctions on the Island of Zanzibar. It is an entirely fitting role for my lifelong hero; Tarzan loathed every variety of unfreedom, every form of captivity, every diminution of the unshackled and soaring human spirit.

I dedicated the book, of course, to my dad, Raymond Donway.

What Is Romanticism, Today?

The Romantic movement in the arts is always evolving. By its nature, as I will explain, it cannot exist without change. For example, today we see writers, filmmakers, and artists winning over new generations to the inspiration and sheer enjoyment of popular Romanticism with works of imagination in the genre called "fantasy."

Literature began the Romantic Revolution in England, specifically the poetry collection, *Lyrical Ballads*, by Samuel Taylor Coleridge and William Wordsworth. (Arguably, Coleridge's "Rime of the Ancient Mariner," included in that collection, remains the greatest poem in the English language.) From the beginning, Romanticism embraced change. The school it replaced was Classicism, which measured all works of art by their adherence to immutable standards defined in Ancient Greece and Rome.

Underlying Romanticism's manifold and often paradoxical themes was the axiom (we would say, "fundamental premise") of free will. In the arts, human volition implied the crucial role of our choice of personal values to guide our lives. That ensured a commitment to change in subject matter and themes as well as in underlying philosophy or "sense of life."

The Romantic revolution is commonly dated from 1780 to 1850, but it continued longer in different countries (e.g., France) and different fields (e.g., music). Perhaps the greatest Romantic writer of all time, French poet, dramatist, and novelist Victor Hugo, published four of his great Romantic novels, including *Les Miserables*, between 1862 and 1874. It was too early for the Nobel Prize in Literature (first awarded in 1901), but his admirer and translator, the legendary Polish novelist, Henryk Sienkiewicz, won the prize in 1905. He was the last Romanticist to be noticed by the Nobel committee.

Philosopher and novelist Ayn Rand, committed to the highest literary expression of Romanticism, acknowledged that by the mid-twentieth-century, Romanticism in serious literature had been supplanted entirely by what she called "Naturalism," but usually is termed "Realism." Among the few exceptions in serious literature are the novels of Ayn Rand, including the modern classics, *The Fountainhead* and *Atlas Shrugged*.

The Romantic Movement in popular "genre" fiction

But even as she kept alive the glory of serious Romantic literature, she acknowledged that as a movement Romanticism had a powerful and continuing presence in "popular" fiction such as detective novels (Agatha Christie, Mickey Spillane), thrillers (Ian Fleming), and other "genre" works. She praised and defended the best of these works as remnants of the Romantic movement favored in the marketplace far more than "serious" literature. She taunted the "literati" who valorized the "common man," but dismissed popular values in fiction such as plot, heroes, a sense of man's efficacy in achieving his values, and black-and-white morality.

Surveying today's scene, we see popular Romanticism gaining everywhere. Detective, thriller, secret agent, science fiction, and other genre novels, usually portraying a hero's triumph against all odds, have never lost their readership. Specific novels remain popular for decades just like, well, "classic" literature. A "classic" is a work that sustains its appeal over generations—and describes many works of Romanticism viewed as "popular," not literary.

Fantasy carries on the Romantic Movement

Arguably, the Romantic genre that has gained the most in recent decades is fantasy. For recent generations, fantasy is as gripping, compulsively readable, inspiring, colorful, and heroic—and as much an invitation to life's struggle for great values—as anything the Romantic tradition has produced.

Certainly, fantasy has been part of Romanticism from the beginning: *Frankenstein* (1818) by Mary Shelley, *The Castle of Otranto* (1764) by Horace Walpole, *Don Juan* (1817) by Lord Byron, *Wuthering Heights* (1847) by Emily Bronte, *Ivanhoe* (1819) by Walter Scott, *The Scarlet Letter* (1850) by Nathaniel Hawthorne, and many more.

Contemporary fantasy, however, is decidedly different and thus difficult to declare "serious literature" even when works are acknowledged as powerful and exceedingly popular. Contemporary fantasy traces its roots to J.R.R. Tolkien, an Oxford scholar of language, literature, and philology who wrote *The Hobbit* (1937) and *The Lord of the Rings: The Fellowship of the Ring* trilogy (1954-55). The *Hobbit* usually is characterized as a book for children.

The Fellowship of the Ring is among the best-selling works of fiction of all time, with more than 150 million copies sold. It is acknowledged to have had a huge effect on modern fantasy, but, like *The Hobbit*, *The Lord of the Rings* has characters that remind one of the best Walt Disney cartoon characters. A library of works now exists arguing for the serious themes, symbols, analogies, mythology, poetry, and inventive philology in Tolkien as well as his implied commentary on religion, the nature of good and evil, death and immortality, German legends, archaeology, and so on. *The Lord of the Rings* trilogy was adapted into three movies (2001-03), all directed by New Zealander Peter Jackson. The first, The Fellowship of the Rings, won four Oscars, and hundreds of other nominations. The international movie database, IMDb, classifies all three movies under the genre: Action, Adventure, and Drama.

Much the same may be said of the works of Tolkien's close friend and associate at Oxford, C. S. Lewis, author of the popular *Chronicles of Narnia* fantasy series. From the seven books, three were adapted—*The Lion, the Witch and the Wardrobe, Prince Caspian,* and *The Voyage of the Dawn Treader*—which collectively grossed over $1.5 billion worldwide.

As suggested, for example, by sales of Tolkien's works, now translated into some 43 languages, the conquest of this new type of fantasy over new generations of readers today has been complete. Fantasy novels are now a huge genre, regular bestsellers, and inspire equally popular big-budget movies and TV series.

What has changed, and greatly, is what "fantasy" means today. There is indeed no shortage of Tolkien imitators—following in his footsteps was British author, J. K. Rowling, with her *Harry Potter* series. Both the huge popularity of her books and their primary audience of young readers remind us of Tolkien.

Beyond the Tolkien-Lewis tradition

But fantasy today has diverged in crucial ways from the Tolkien-Lewis-Rowling tradition. As I have said, this field of fiction is huge and active, so "anything" may be found in it, but I will comment on a few of my favorite fantasy novels that also happen to be big bestsellers and even household names.

Among my favorites, to date, are the *Game of Thrones* series; the trilogy *The Hunger Games;* the novels of Patrick Rothfuss, *The Name of the Wind,* and The Wise Man's Fear; and a few other bestsellers. My purpose, when I began, was to explore a new Romantic genre. Very soon, I was turning the pages as compulsively as any other reader enjoying the "escape"—but, in reality, "inspiration"—of Romantic literature. Romantic fiction presents readers with *more* difficult, urgent, and crucial struggles than "real life."

In *The Name of the Wind* (2007), Kvothe, orphaned and alone as a child, facing an often-brutal world, creates his character, his chances in life, and his exultant adventures. The moral fundamentals never change. He comes from the most rejected and despised "minority" of the era—the equivalent of the European gypsies, in our time—and triumphs not only as an individual but in the name of redeeming his people, the Edema Ruh. There is little in this novel that is "generic." In whatever role Kvothe finds himself—child beggar, university student, musician, scientist, lover, or warrior—the action is sophisticated and complex.

One intriguing comment on fantasy novels insists that the defining characteristic of the genre is a "magic system." That is true in Tolkien, C.S. Lewis, George Martin, and Patrick Rothfuss. Perhaps more interesting still is that the shortlist of characteristics of fantasy fiction includes a "power structure/system of government." In Tolkien and Lewis, that is not a factor. In all contemporary fantasy fiction I have read it has been a factor. It represents the core conflict in *The Hunger Games.*

It would be interesting to compare this novel and its sequel with some great Romantic "literary" novels. Usually, such novels differ from the popular in the seriousness of their themes, depth of psychology, and effectiveness of writing style. But to that must be added, I think, the criterion of complexity, especially the subtlety and novelty of conflicts. By that criterion, Rothfuss can present, although not consistently, a challenge to any "serious" Romantic literature.

I am new to fantasy literature as a genre (although I was long ago a fan of the *Narnia* series) and not prepared to comment on the issue of style as differentiating "serious" from "popular" fiction not only in Romanticism but Realism. I enjoyed the style of *Game of Thrones, Hunger Games,* and the two Rothfuss novels. I think that for the enjoyment of style as such, not only style as an indispensable tool, the Rothfuss novels kept arresting me to attend to style.

The hugely popular series by George R.R. Martin, *Song of Fire and Ice* (often referred to by the title of the first book, *Game of Thrones*), has spawned five novels since 1991 (each more than 1,000 pages). Taking for its setting an entire world of countries, peoples, castles, kings, powerful ruling families, dragons, and murderous spirits of the dead, *Song of Fire and Ice* ultimately follows hundreds of characters. The challenges Martin conjures up for these characters are always life- and sanity-threatening. The extravagance of invention, which Ayn Rand always characterized as "inexhaustible" in Romanticists, is George Martin's trademark—and nowhere as evident as in his cast of heroes.

There is nothing peculiarly "for young readers," here, with horrifying descriptions of violence, disease, torture, and poverty, and also not-very-restrained language. But typical of Romanticism, the characters are unique and colorful—larger than life heroes and villains—and the plot sustains suspense for thousands of pages. This series, of course, goes right back to one of the earliest and strongest traditions of the Romantic era: the portrayal of a nobler time of knights and ladies. There is plenty of that in *Song of Fire and Ice*, but with equal time for medieval horrors of murder, mutilation, and nightmare cruelty—in case you are looking for the struggle between good and evil.

The Hunger Games trilogy (2008-10), by Suzanne Collins, felt to me like a pure Romantic literary experience. It also had for me the intrigue of a dystopian novel of dictatorship and rebellion against it. Katniss Everdeen, 16 years old in the first book, is a Romantic heroine. I cannot imagine a young reader, today, not responding to her unstudied heroism, the assumption that she will fight against anything—including the surreal dictatorship—for her life and personal values.

The author, to me, makes it believable that in the end she wins, bringing down the existing dictatorship—and then putting an arrow in the heart of the new "freedom leader" who suddenly proposes continuing the worst practices of the dictatorship. Emotionally, I bought it all. That is the imagination and skill, the craft, of top Romanticist authors. This trilogy is categorized as "young adult," a huge sub-genre, but I swear that YA, here, means only that the sex is limited to kissing. These novels are no more inherently limited in readership than *Lord of the Flies*, which, after all, is exclusively about teenage characters.

I am not surprised that *The Game of Thrones* series and *The Hunger Games* trilogy became TV sensations. Where on TV, today, do we find genuine heroes (imaginative *or* real), conflicts over crucial values, the portrayal of the world as inexhaustibly exciting, and battles that are agonizing but ultimately successful (and worth winning)?

Escapism?

Return to one of my favorite characters, Kvothe. He is born to the Edema Ruh, wandering performers of the lowest social status who automatically are accused of any theft, kidnapping, horse rustling. After his family is murdered by demons (this is fantasy), he survives, overcomes all obstacles to get an education, and becomes a magician, musician, and warrior—but never forgets his origins.

As a man, traveling through a forest, he encounters what he believes at first is a tribe of Edema Ruh. He soon perceives that they are bandits who killed a band of Edema Ruh and took their wagons. At a village performance, they lured away two girls that now are repeatedly raped.

When he realizes this, Kvothe poisons the dinner pot. He demands he get the two girls for the night but puts them in his tent and sleeps outside on guard. When he hears the bandits moaning and crying out from the poison, he stalks them and kills them all. Then, he brings the girls, wagons, horses, and all goods and money of the bandits back to the village where the girls live.

He endures attacks by the villagers who accuse him of abducting the girls. That is quickly halted when the girls, enraged, ask why the villagers did not rescue them but Kvothe did?

Having returned the girls and given their families everything, Kvothe gets ready to leave. The mayor of the village suddenly asks: "But can't we do something for *you*?"

Kvothe answers: "Remember it was bandits who took them… And remember it was one of the Edema Ruh who brought them back." (*The Wise Man's Fear*)

New Romanticists writing fantasy do not dodge issues such as collectivism versus individualism. Or the brutality of dictatorships that view individuals like Katniss Everdeen as mere pawns. If this is "escapism," it is an escape from helpless submergence in the masses to become, like Katniss Everdeen, ready to combat an evil dictatorship to protect [herself and?] those she loves.

Ayn Rand turned to fantasy (specifically, dystopia in her novella,

Anthem, to dramatize certain ideas. The fantasy involved, however, is wholly traditional, not contemporary in the sense we discussed. The singular theme is the individual mind, the engine of all human progress, trapped in a world of collectivist submergence of any hint of individuality. In the final analysis, that is the power of fantasy in fiction: It can create a world that starkly, without ambiguity or even nuance, pits values against each other.

In fiction, the border between fantasy and "reality" is not easy to locate. (After all, "fiction" means not factual.) Ayn Rand deemed Victor Hugo's novel, *The Man Who Laughs*, set in late seventeenth-century England, the greatest novel in world literature. It also is the Hugo novel closest to fantasy, with one lead character who is remarkably like Kvothe.

Those who have kept alive their ability to respond to the individual's struggle to achieve his or her values (and children most often begin with that perspective) will thrill to the growing—and changing—Romantic literature of fantasy.

ABOUT THE AUTHOR

Walter Donway discovered the novels of Ayn Rand during the summer between high school and college, in 1962, reading *Atlas Shrugged* first. His brother, Roger, and he became lifelong students and advocates of Objectivism. They met David Kelley while students at Brown University.

Walter attended many speeches by Ayn Rand at Ford Hall Forum, in Boston, and live lectures at the Nathaniel Branden Institute in New York City.

When David Kelley launched the Institute of Objectivist Studies, in 1990, which today is The Atlas Society, he asked Walter to be a trustee. He remained on the board of trustees for 20 years, until 2010, and, among other contributions, founded and edited its first publication, *The IOS Journal*.

Walter has contributed articles to all publications of the Atlas Society and its predecessor organizations, including *The IOS Journal, Navigator, The New Individualist*, and the commentary section of the TAS Web site. He made presentations, including the original form of several essays in this book, at the TAS Summer Seminars.

He is the author of three volumes of poetry, the first published by the Atlas Society; four novels; and nonfiction works including *Not Half Free: The Myth That America Is Capitalist*, with a preface by David Kelley, and, most recently, *Donald Trump and His Enemies: How the Media Put Trump in Office*. He has published a memoir of growing up, *"You're Probably from Holden, If...": Growing Up in A Vanishing New England*.

His articles have been published in the *Wall Street Journal, Cosmopolitan, Medical World News, Human Events, Private Practice,* the *Iowa Review*, and other periodicals.

At present, he lives in New York City and East Hampton, NY. In addition to his literary work, he is a fund-raising communications consultant to nonprofit organizations. He is roving editor of the online site, "Savvy Street," founded and edited by Objectivist Vinay Kolhatkar, where more than 60 of his articles on contemporary affairs have been published.

Acknowledgments

Thanks, here, to Donna Paris for editing the original version of this book as she has edited many of my other books. Thanks to Vinay Kolhatkar for accepting, editing, and publishing many of these chapters first in *Savvy Street*. Thanks to the Atlas Society, also, for publishing the originals of many of these chapters.

Thanks to my son, Ethan Donway, for many productive discussions of the fantasy genre—his generation's popular Romantic literature. And to Roger Donway, for discussions now far too numerous, far-reaching, and inspiring to acknowledge specifically. In poetry, as in so many subjects discussed here, he has been my "seminar."

I painfully miss the weeklong summer seminars of the Atlas Society and its precursors, the Institute of Objectivist Studies and the Objectivist Institute, where all these ideas and so much more were proposed, debated, refined, and articulated. If an angel should read these words, the seminars could exist again, in style, for $100,000 a year—and named, of course, for the philanthropist. I often felt, as the week went on, that my flight had been diverted to Galt's Gulch. It was that good! And attendees, by the way, always were ready to pay their share.

Thanks to David Kelley, who, with all the demands on his time, took on writing the preface to this book. From the moment I read *Atlas Shrugged*, I knew I would spend my life telling the world about it. David's courageous and life-saving decision to create an organization for "open Objectivism"—a term coined later—gave me my best chance.

Our Work

Publications: From graphic novels to pocket guides, our books are available in multiple formats and languages.

Narrative Videos: From animation to comedic features, our productions include *Draw My Life* videos and graphic novel-style compilations.

Educational Resources: Online courses, podcasts, webinars, campus speaking tours, living-history presentations, and campus activism projects are among the wealth of ways we educate students of all ages about reason, achievement, individualism, and freedom.

Student Programs: Our Atlas Advocates are eager, curious, and thoughtful students and young professionals who meet for monthly book club discussions, and The Atlas Society Senior Scholar Richard Salsman, Ph.D.'s Morals & Markets webinar course.

Our Atlas Intellectuals are adults who meet monthly to bring Ayn Rand's philosophy to bear on current events and real-world topics as curated by The Atlas Society Senior Scholar Stephen Hicks, Ph.D.

Commentaries: In addition to educational resources, our website offers commentaries on a wide range of political, cultural, and personal topics and events.

The Atlas Society is a 501(c)3 nonprofit organization. For additional information, or to support our work, please contact us via email info@atlassociety.org or via our website atlassociety.org.

22001 Northpark Drive, Ste 250 Kingwood, TX | 77339 United States

Made in the USA
Columbia, SC
28 September 2021